INTERCULTURAL COUPLES

INTERCULTURAL COUPLES

Crossing Boundaries,
Negotiating Difference

Jill M. Bystydzienski

NEW YORK UNIVERSITY PRESS
New York and London

NEW YORK UNIVERSITY PRESS
New York and London
www.nyupress.org

© 2011 by New York University
All rights reserved

References to Internet websites (URLs) were accurate at the time of writing. Neither the author nor New York University Press is responsible for URLs that may have expired or changed since the manuscript was prepared.

Library of Congress Cataloging-in-Publication Data

Bystydzienski, Jill M., 1949–
Intercultural couples : crossing boundaries, negotiating difference / Jill M. Bystydzienski.
p. cm.
Includes bibliographical references and index.
ISBN 978–0–8147–9978–9 (cl : alk. paper) — ISBN 978–0–8147–9979–6 (pb : alk. paper) — ISBN 978–0–8147–0947–4 (ebook)
1. Interethnic marriage. 2. Intercountry marriage 3. Cultural relations. 4. Interracial marriage. 5. Racially mixed people. I. Title.
HQ1031.B97   2011
306.84′50973—dc22   2010048337

New York University Press books are printed on acid-free paper, and their binding materials are chosen for strength and durability. We strive to use environmentally responsible suppliers and materials to the greatest extent possible in publishing our books.

Manufactured in the United States of America
c 10 9 8 7 6 5 4 3 2 1
p 10 9 8 7 6 5 4 3 2 1

For my daughter, Katy

Contents

	Acknowledgments	ix
	Introduction	1
1	The Couples	17
2	Reinventing Cultural Identity in Intergroup Couple Relationships	45
3	Differences That Matter Within Couple Relationships	81
4	Differences That Matter Across Relationships	111
5	Accommodating Differences	137
	Conclusion	165
	Methodological Appendix: A Feminist Approach to Interviewing	177
	List of Study Participants	186
	Notes	189
	Bibliography	193
	Index	207
	About the Author	213

Acknowledgments

Like all scholarly projects, this book would not have been possible without the help and support of many people. I am eternally grateful to the couples who agreed to be interviewed and who shared so generously with me their accounts of their lives together. My colleague and friend Estelle Resnik conducted about half of the interviews and transcribed many of them. Initially, Franklin College of Indiana provided two substantial faculty development grants for transcriptions, and Iowa State University made available additional funds for the completion of the final transcripts.

Throughout the process of writing this book my life partner, Hal Pepinsky, read chapter drafts and gave me, as always, his unconditional support. I am thankful to colleagues Donna Eder, Tracey Owens Patton, and the late Steven Schacht, who read chapters and provided valuable feedback, and to two anonymous reviewers who gave me excellent suggestions for revisions. Gary Dunham provided his invaluable editing expertise in the last phase of the project. Ilene Kalish, executive editor at NYU Press, has been wonderful to work with. I greatly appreciated her encouragement throughout the project and am especially grateful to her for giving me generous contract extensions when I had to postpone delivery of the manuscript due to my move to The Ohio State University.

Finally, I want to thank all of the people, too numerous to mention, who have expressed genuine interest in this project and whose comments, questions, and advice motivated me to continue with the book and to complete it after many years. Their gentle urging kept me returning to the task, often with a new perspective, mining the rich interviews for fruitful analysis and significant findings.

Introduction

Diverse populations in the United States have interacted increasingly during the last several decades, despite the persistence of racial segregation, ethnic antagonism, and anti-immigration sentiments. Cross-cultural, cross-racial, and international contacts have grown tremendously, facilitated by the breaking down of legal and cultural restrictions to interracial marriage, by affirmative action—which expands the opportunity for meeting people of diverse backgrounds in the workplace, and by technological advances that make possible greater mobility and communication around the globe. A rapidly growing consequence of this increasing contact is intercultural couples: domestic partnerships comprised of partners from different ethnic, racial, religious, or national backgrounds.

Although accurate statistics concerning such persons married to or living with each other in the United States are not readily available, existing data as well as estimates suggest that intercultural couples may well number in the tens of millions (Clemetson 2000; U.S. Census Bureau 2008a; 2008b). During the 1980s and 1990s, out-marriage rates for European American groups, for American Indians, and for African Americans in the United States increased significantly; intermarriage between Catholics and Protestants, Jews and Gentiles, and between persons of different class backgrounds and educational levels also grew (Kalmijn 1998). As new immigration from Asia and Latin America has increased racial and ethnic diversity in the United States, rates of intermarriage between racial and ethnic groups have risen concurrently (Lee and Bean 2004). Demographic changes in family structure involving an increasing number of individuals experiencing "the independent life stage," or living on their own, traveling, and supporting themselves, are also connected to establishing more "nontraditional unions" (Rosenfeld 2007).

The multilayered experiences of such "nontraditional" intergroup couples—heterosexual as well as same-sex unions—are thrown into relief in the pages that follow, drawing largely upon dozens of in-depth interviews with persons living in mixed domestic partnerships representing a broad spectrum of ethnic, racial, religious, socioeconomic, and national backgrounds. Despite the growing presence of intercultural couples in the United States and worldwide, they remain an understudied phenomenon. The few studies of intergroup partnerships to date have been relatively restricted in scope, concerned mostly with interracial couples (Bratter and King 2008; Childs 2005; Forry, Leslie, and Letiecq 2007; Fu 2008; Gullickson 2006; Johnson and Warren 1994; Kennedy 2004; McNamara, Tempenis, and Walton 1999; Root 1992; 2001; Rosenblatt, Karis, and Powell 1995; Stuart and Abt 1993; Wilkerson 1991; Yancey and Lewis 2009; Zhang and Van Hook 2009), interfaith marriage (Berman 1968; Curtis and Ellison 2002; Glaser 1997; Kaplan 2004; Lazerwitz 1995; Lee 1994; McGinity 2008; Medding 1992; Monahan 1973; Romano 2003), or international couples (Grearson and Smith 2001, 1995; Romano 1988; Thornton 1992).

Intercultural couples pivot on the interaction of people of different backgrounds at the level of personal intimacy in daily life. In this context, where the influence of intimacy provides a field of nurture and conflict, it is possible to see how members of various ethnic, racial, national, and religious groups, as well as people of different genders and sexual orientations, perceive and respond to social differences. Each partner brings a different set of cultural experiences to the relationship that may include gender expectations, ideas about appropriate relations with family members, childrearing, general lifestyle, and even language. Sometimes the differences may be unrecognized or seen as minimal. In the process of everyday life some differences, however, can become salient, forming the basis for conflict, enriching diversity, or both (Breger and Hill 1998). Those differences regarded as problematic are then negotiated by the partners in the course of their daily lives together. Negotiations of difference take place at two levels—between the partners in the couple relationship, and between the couple and individuals and groups outside the partnership (e.g., family members, acquaintances, people in the community or neighborhood). These types of negotiations are sometimes openly acknowledged in discussions and sometimes more implicit arrangements and accommodations are worked out without explicit articulation.

Which dimensions of difference matter more to such couples and which are regarded as less important? Which differences are significant to those outside of the couple relationships? How do the couple partners accommodate themselves to the differences that are most problematic for them? In which ways do intimate daily intercultural exchanges affect the identities of the partners and their joint identity as a couple? How are cultural identities created and maintained in these relationships? These key questions both guide and emerge from the study.

A Word About Words

Since this study deals centrally with "culture"—a very broad, contested concept that has been used variously by scholars and lay persons alike—it is important to explain clearly how it is employed in this book. Additionally, other potentially problematic terms such as *gender, class, race, ethnicity, social difference,* and *background* need to be defined because they appear frequently in the chapters that follow and carry various meanings both in academic circles and the wider world.

Culture is defined here as the social heritage, including values (beliefs, aspirations, common understandings), norms (rules of conduct), and practices (what people do and say), assumed to be shared by a group with which individuals identify. Cultural identification is a complex concept that involves assuming certain cultural identities over others (Ahmed 2000), and what constitutes a "different" culture from one's own may not be easy to define or recognize. Although it often appears that a group of people has a clear idea of whom or what belongs and does not belong, on closer examination the dividing line is fluid; moreover, definitions can change significantly over time (Breger and Hill 1998). As Uma Narayan (2000) points out, cultures are often represented "as if they were entities that exist neatly distinct and separate in the world...obscuring the reality that boundaries between them are human constructs, underdetermined by existing variations in worldviews and ways of life" (1084).

While my understanding of *culture* does not concur with popular renderings of the term that tend to present cultural groups as clearly distinct from one another, in this study I relied on the perceptions of the participants regarding cultural differences between them and their partners rather than trying to determine myself to what extent cultural differences between them existed. Thus, while I recognize that cultures are not unitary and that it is problematic to distinguish the groups with which one feels affiliation from others that appear "different," nevertheless it is important to acknowledge that such perceptions are part of daily life, and especially the lives of couple partners who are assumed to come from two very different worlds. As this study shows, by living intimately with those the couple partners initially perceived to be from different cultures, they come to see that the boundaries between cultures are not impermeable and that commonalities exist across groups they may have once regarded as entirely distinct.

The term "intercultural"[1] seems appropriate to characterize these couples, as most of the recognized dimensions of difference between the partners—gender, class, religion, nationality, and even race (which is socially constructed and often confounded with ethnicity)—intersect with culture. *Gender*, or the socially defined expectations for female and male persons (what are sometimes termed "gender roles") as well as a system of socially structured power relations between women and men,[2] derives its content from the cultural contexts within which people are located. *Class*, typically defined as a social category based on income, education, and/or lifestyle, intersects with culture because cultural sites influence how people perceive social classes and deal with their consequences.[3] *Religion* encompasses beliefs, shared understandings, and rituals that are part of a society's culture within which they develop and operate. *Nationality* or the status of belonging to a particular nation-state is always tied to cultural understandings that are implicit in the spatially defined or imagined national entity (Yuval-Davis 1997).

Race is commonly employed to denote phenotypic categories of humans based on specific physical markers (e.g., skin color, hair texture, and/or facial features). In the United States, there is the problematic perception that five distinct racial groups exist: Asian, Black, Hispanic/Latino/a, Native American, and White, each with its specific phenotypic traits. I understand *race* to be a social construction, meaning that there are no inherent biological or phenotypic characteristics that, taken together, constitute a particular "race" of people, but rather that human beings actively create racial categories within specific cultural contexts that vary across time and place for a variety of reasons (Ferrante and Brown 2001; Haney-Lopez 1995; Omi and Winant 1986). I find useful George M. Fredrickson's (1988) definition of race as a "consciousness of status and identity based on ancestry and color" (12). Since many of the participants of this study defined race primarily in reference to skin color and used the five categories (plus an additional one referring to Middle Eastern Arabs as persons of color) to identify themselves and others, I have employed this socially constructed definition and categories of "race" accordingly in this book. While I refer to couple partners as "Asian," "Black," "Latina/o," or "White," these terms are understood to correspond to social groups rather than biologically distinct categories of human beings.

The term *ethnicity* is often used synonymously with *culture*. It refers to shared beliefs and patterns of behavior, including a perceived common ancestry, an assumed shared historical past, and symbolic elements such as kinship patterns or nationality, as well as a consciousness of kind among members of the group. Additionally, phenotypic markers are also frequently associated with an ethnic group (Spickard 1989, 12). In this book, I use *ethnicity* to refer to specific U.S. cultural groups such as African Americans or Polish Americans, while I employ the term *culture* more broadly when referring to social group differences.

Social difference, a phrase that appears frequently throughout the book, refers to difference between the couple partners that they or I attribute to the social categories of gender, race, ethnicity, class, religion, and nationality. *Social difference* is thus distinct from individual or interpersonal difference where, for example, partners might recognize a dissimilarity between them in personalities or idiosyncratic preferences for certain types of interests, tasks, or activities.

Finally, I employ the term *background* to refer to social categories of origin that the couple partners bring to their relationships. Hence, when discussing the social class of partners, I discuss the *background* socioeconomic status of the study participants (the class into which they were born and in which they were raised) and distinguish it from their current class standing. Background characteristics of partners may also include the type of family in which they grew up (e.g., two-parent or single-parent), the religion in which they were raised (e.g., Catholic or Muslim), and the type of location in which they lived (e.g., a small village, medium-size town, or large city).

Previous Studies of Intergroup Couples

Until recently, most studies of intergroup couples have tended to portray such relationships in decidedly negative terms. Intermarriage and ethnically and racially mixed couples have been typically labeled as problematic (e.g., Barron 1972; Levine and Rhodes 1981; Spickard 1989), assumed to be inherently difficult to maintain, and more often in need of intervention and counseling than endogamous (in-group) relationships (e.g., Gaines and Ickes 1997; Ibrahim and Schroeder 1990; Smith 1996).

Social scientists and others have studied intergroup couples from a variety of perspectives; most have focused on why and how some people choose partners from other than their own social groups, and the consequences of such unions. Some (sociologists in particular) have attempted to explain why individuals date and marry across cultural/racial lines, often citing socioeconomic factors such as income and education. For example, in a sexist model of "compensatory hypogamy" (Breger and Hill 1998, 16) in heterosexual relationships, white low-income and "unattractive" women who marry men of color are presumed to do so in order to benefit from their husbands' higher socioeconomic status, while men of color who marry white women presumably benefit from their wives' racial status (Kalmijn 1998; Merton 1941; Muhsam 1990). Other researchers have examined which groups are more open to intermarriage, finding, for instance, that first generation immigrants are much less likely to intermix with other groups than are second or third immigrant generations (Barron 1972; Lee and Yamanaka 1990), or discovering that college-educated, intellectually and artistically inclined people are more likely than others to choose partners from social groups different from their own (Barron 1972; Gordon 1964). Some social scientists have argued that the marriage of women out of certain groups is often more strictly controlled and regulated than that of men (Abdulrahim 1993; Barbara 1989; Buijs 1993). Still others have viewed intergroup couples and marriage as a form of assimilation, a process by which a minority group loses its distinct ethnic identity (Alba 1986; Barron 1972; Ellman 1971; Gordon 1964; Kennedy 1952; Levine and Rhodes 1981; Murguia and Frisbie 1977). Researchers who approach the subject from psychological perspectives have emphasized socioemotional influences such as love and esteem on exogamous (out-group) mate selection (e.g., Gaines and Liu 2000; Staples and Johnson 1993).

Such previous research has tended to approach intergroup couples either from the "outside," by focusing on general structural and cultural patterns responsible for the choice of exogamous partnerships and the consequences of these choices, or by locating the basis of such partner selection in individual emotional states. For the most part, these studies have neglected to elucidate the dynamics of the relationship between the partners within the couple as well as the couple's relations with others outside the domestic partnership.

However, in the last two decades, there has been a growing focus on the *experiences* of the persons in intercultural couples and thus on understanding such relationships from the perspective of the partners themselves (see, e.g., Childs 2005; Diggs 2001; Forry, Leslie, and Letiecq 2007; Grearson and Smith 2001, 1995; Johnson and Warren 1994; Kellner 2009; Root 2001). Such approaches to intergroup unions have provided at once more sympathetic views of these relationships and more balanced portrayals in which both the problems and the triumphs of the couples are presented side by side. As the more recent studies demonstrate, many intercultural relationships beat the odds and survive over time (Bratter and King 2008; Frame 2004; Zhang and Van Hook 2009). Moreover, the quality of intercultural couple relationships has been shown to be similar to or even higher on some dimensions (e.g., relationship satisfaction) than their intracultural counterparts (Leslie and Letiecq 2004; Reiter and Gee 2008; Troy, Lewis-Smith, and Laurenceau 2006).

It is important to remember that existing studies of intergroup couples focus almost exclusively on heterosexual relationships and on legally married couples.[4] Absent from such studies are heterosexual couples choosing to cohabit without marriage and an increasing number of gay men and lesbians establishing domestic partnerships. Analyses that exclude such partnerships can only develop partial explanations about intercultural couples. Consequently, the sample of couples interviewed for the present study includes both cohabiting heterosexual and same-sex couples.[5] Throughout this book, I frequently use the term "domestic partnerships" to encompass all of these couples (married, cohabiting, heterosexual, and same-sex), as it is a broad, neutral category that, when employed in this way, also normalizes couple relationships usually associated with nonheterosexuals.

A Conceptual Framework for Studying Intercultural Couples

The conceptual perspective I employ in this book derives from feminist approaches to the study of interpersonal relationships and builds on those more recent studies of intergroup couples that focus on experiences and perceptions of the partners inside their couple relationships.[6] It also draws on the developing area of feminist research on difference, scholarship that seeks productive ways of theorizing race, class, gender, and sexuality (Archer 2004; Chancer and Watkins 2006; Hesse-Biber and Yaiser 2004; Kitch 2009; Wanzo 2009).

Feminist scholars often conduct in-depth studies of individuals and groups and emphasize the importance of the subjectivity of their research participants (Bell 2009; Bloom 1998; Bondi et al. 2002; Carpenter 2005; Collins 1990; Litt 2000). They propose that people who take part in the research present their reality to the researcher from their own perspectives, thus revealing the meanings the phenomenon under study has for the participants. This approach provides the opportunity for those whose voices historically have been suppressed (usually women and members of various minority groups) to tell their own stories, which the researcher then attempts fairly and accurately to present in her/his work. As I indicated above, those who recently have begun to study intergroup couples from the standpoint of the partners living within these relationships have dispelled false assumptions about such couples made previously by researchers who used more traditional approaches. The subjective approach is as important, or even more so, for the study of intercultural couples within which partners diverge on several social dimensions simultaneously, struggle to create new identities, and seek ways to deal

Introduction

with multiple layers of difference. It would be impossible to understand the dynamics of these couple relationships without exploring how the individuals involved made personal sense of their lives together.

The new feminist scholarship on difference seeks to explicate the complex relations between its multiple dimensions. There are several aspects of this approach that are particularly relevant to my study of intercultural couples. First, race, class, gender, sexuality, and nationality are socially constructed categories, carrying meanings and interpretations created through struggles between groups, the dominant group having the power to define these categories and to institutionalize a system of social ranking (Chancer and Watkins 2006; Ferrante and Brown 2001; Weber 2004). Because these categories are created socially, they are not permanent and natural, and people are able to change their significance. As the findings of my study show, in intercultural couples, the significance of societal inequalities that partners bring to these relationships, such as those of race and gender, can be transformed in the process of building relatively equal partnerships.

A second aspect of the new feminist scholarship on difference is the analysis of how race, class, gender, and sexuality intersect or operate simultaneously (Bystydzienski and Aulette 1990). As many have argued, at the structural (macro) level, hierarchies of difference are interconnected and present in all institutions (work organizations, schools, families, etc.), while individuals exist at different locations (micro level) along the dimensions (of race, class, gender, and sexuality), all of which are assumed to have similar importance (Collins 1995; King 1990; Moya 1997; Weber 2004; West and Fernstermaker 1995). Some feminist scholars, however, question the idea that all social differences are inextricably interwoven and equally important to individuals; in some contexts certain differences may not be significant while other differences become salient (e.g., Barvosa-Carter 2001; Hurtado 2003; Takagi 1996; Ward 2004). This latter approach is particularly relevant to my study, as the intercultural couples interviewed here make a clear distinction between those dimensions of difference that do and do not matter to them and those that matter to persons and groups outside the couple.

Third, it is not enough to examine race, class, gender, and sexuality solely as macro social structures working as interlocking systems of oppression, but also to understand how they operate on the micro or social psychological level of interpersonal relationships (Frye 1983; Weber 2004). People internalize social oppression differently and develop different approaches for dealing with problems that stem from oppression. For instance, in my study I found that couple partners have internalized class oppression more deeply than other dimensions of difference; also, intercultural couples develop a variety of accommodations to those dimensions of difference that they consider salient.

Finally, some feminist scholars focusing on difference have examined the realities of persons who occupy social locations that resist categorization (Anzaldua 1987; Lenz 2004; Rowe and Licona 2005; Moya 2001). Those who cross cultures (e.g., move from one country to another or establish personal relationships with people of different social backgrounds) or who embody multiple differences (e.g., biracial or multiracial/ethnic individuals) often do not see themselves as "belonging" to specific groups but rather as residing in "in-between" (Bhabha 1994; Fountas 2005; Walter 2003) or "third" (Rowe and Licona 2005) spaces from which they develop new, hybrid identities and establish innovative sites of collaboration and contestation. This perspective is highly useful for understanding intercultural couples whose identities are constructed subjectively by the partners out of the interrelations among gender, race, ethnicity, class, religion, and nationality and the blurring of boundaries between them. Intercultural couple partnerships can thus be conceived as border crossing between multiple categories of social difference.

Method and Sample

I used a qualitative research method—in-depth personal interviews—to study intercultural couples. Qualitative methods are most appropriate for the investigation of close relationship processes such as relational maintenance and conflict (Allen and Walker 2000). In-depth interviews allowed me to access the processes by which couple partners negotiated meaning and from their own perspectives made sense of their lives together.

I and a colleague, Estelle Resnik, conducted interviews for this study with thirty-five couples between 1995 and 2000.[7] Couples had to satisfy two criteria before being chosen to be interviewed. First, they had to have been living together (whether married or not) for at least two years. It was important that the couples selected would have had the opportunity to experience life in a domestic partnership over time. I judged that two years was a reasonable minimal time for a couple to begin to develop a shared history. Second, the partners needed to differ on at least two social dimensions: ethnicity, nationality, race, class, or religion. Although a significant number of the couple partners were born in a non-English speaking country or grew up bilingual,[8] language was not chosen as a dimension of possible difference between them. By the time the study participants were interviewed they were all fluent in English, the international partners having lived in the United States for at least three years, and used the English language to communicate with each other.[9]

I also included in my sample the written and published self-narratives of three intercultural couples (Brown and Farahyar 1994; Johnson and Johnson 1994; Tartakov and Tartakov 1994). Remarkably, these first-person narratives closely resemble the in-depth interviews, as each of the partners provides a separate account of the couple relationship and they engage in most of the questions and issues discussed with the interview participants. One of the couple narratives also includes a joint account written by both partners (Tartakov and Tartakov 1994). The three couples met the criteria for selection for the interviews.

Intercultural couples who had separated or were divorced were not selected for this study. The focus of the study is on the processes by which couple partners who live together on a daily basis recognize and negotiate social difference, how they perceive changes in their identities as a result of being in intercultural relationships, and how they communicate and deal with potential conflict. The participation of *intact* couples thus has been central to this project.

Whether or not the couples had children was also not a selection criterion, given the focus on the couple relationships.[10] When interviewing those with children, however, questions were asked about childrearing practices and the couples were given an opportunity to explore whether and how their differing cultural backgrounds influenced their attitudes toward and relations with children. The three couple narratives included partners' reflections on childrearing and relationships with their children.

A snowball sampling technique was employed to construct the sample of interviewees in which, at first, a few persons having the required characteristics were identified and interviewed, and they in turn identified others who qualified for inclusion in the sample. From the names obtained, those least closely connected to the referring individuals were selected in order to minimize bias. To avoid obtaining a skewed sample in terms of socioeconomic, educational, and family background, we attempted to choose the respondents to represent a cross-section of the U.S. population. However, as middle-class academics, we were more successful in obtaining interviews with well-educated, middle-class intercultural couples than poor or working-class couples. Nonetheless, the final sample included more than 50 percent of couples where one of the partners' class of origin was lower or working, and close to 20 percent of the individuals held blue-collar or service jobs at the time of the interviews. Referrals for intercultural same-sex couples were obtained through several lesbian and gay networks. Six of the thirty-eight couples (15 percent) included in the study were in same-sex unions. (For further breakdown of the sample in terms of the various dimensions of social difference, see chapter 1.)

We chose the snowball sampling strategy because it allowed access to couples who would have been difficult or impossible to interview without referrals from those they knew. This sampling technique is often used to select participants from "hidden populations" (Browne 2005; Carlson et al. 1994; Lopes, Rodrigues, and Sichieri 1996), when the population under investigation is not visible due to either low numbers or not fitting the hegemonic norm (in this study's case, the norm of in-group and, for some of the study participants, heterosexual coupling).

Snowball sampling has been used successfully by numerous researchers to select participants for in-depth interviews in a variety of social settings.[11] The snowball technique does not yield representative samples but, as this study attests, it does not preclude the selection of a very diverse group of participants.[12]

While my sample consists of thirty-eight couples (seventy individual interviews and six self-narratives), data saturation was reached at about thirty couples, after which responses to interview questions became repetitive and did not add significant new themes in the data. It is, of course, impossible to generalize from this relatively small sample to all intercultural couples in the United States and this is not the purpose of the study. Rather, this study joins a substantial body of previous works that made use of relatively small samples to obtain interview data and propose findings that reveal the rich complexity of people's lives.[13]

In-depth, audiotaped interviews were conducted in person with almost all of the seventy respondents.[14] Initial interviews with ten couples identified through referrals took place in south-central Indiana; subsequent interviews were held in Massachusetts, Pennsylvania, New Jersey, Florida, California, Minnesota, and Iowa.[15] Each partner in the couple was interviewed separately in order to obtain responses uninfluenced by the presence of the other partner. Previous research in which married or cohabiting couples were interviewed demonstrates the importance of separate interviews, as each partner tends to have a different view of the couple relationship (Bernard 1972; Diggs 2001; Rubin 1976; 1995; Wajcman 1983; Zinn and Eitzen 1996, 251–54). The respondents were asked questions about their backgrounds, how they met, what attracted them to each other, what cultural and other differences (if any) they perceived between themselves and their partners, how they were made aware of and how they dealt with these differences, and how their views of themselves were affected by having a partner from a different social group.

As explained in more detail in the appendix, I and my colleague attempted to interview the respondents in a way that would honestly and fairly represent their own realities. The questions were open-ended and we encouraged the study participants to speak as long as they wished, occasionally probing or asking for clarification. As respondents and interviewers were drawn into mutual engagement, the interviews often turned interestingly into conversations. Lasting an hour to two hours, the audiotaped interviews were subsequently transcribed. All the names of the participants who were interviewed have been changed and some aspects of their social backgrounds, occupations, and locations altered to preserve confidentiality.[16]

I have reason to believe that my personal background helped in conducting the interviews. My interest in this topic developed out of experiences of having crossed cultures several times in childhood and early adulthood, and having lived in an intercultural domestic partnership for more than thirty years. I spent the first eight years of my life in Poland, then lived with my parents and sister in New York City for five years, and subsequently spent ten years with my family of origin in the French Canadian province of Quebec. I married an American who grew up mainly in the U.S. Midwest, whose father was of Russian Jewish background and whose mother is an Anglo-American (nonpracticing) Christian from the U.S. South. My partner and I struggled with substantial differences of culture and economic class, especially during the early years of our marriage. Although this personal experience did not give me a definitive understanding of intercultural couples, it proved valuable in developing rapport with the participants of this study. The couples I telephoned or emailed seldom turned down my requests for interviews after I explained that I was also part of an intercultural couple. I believe that knowing of my similar experience helped the respondents be more open with me regarding their intimate lives together.

When analyzing the interviews and narratives, I first identified prevalent themes and then reread the transcripts to determine the presence or absence of each theme in an individual interview or narrative.[17] Throughout my analysis and its presentation in this book, I relied heavily on the words and first-hand perceptions of the participants; their own perspectives were essential for understanding the processes by which they recognized and negotiated the differences between themselves and their partners. Nevertheless, the analysis and interpretation of their viewpoints are ultimately mine.

A more detailed consideration of methodological issues that arose while conducting the interviews is explored in the appendix. I discuss ethical concerns, the advantages of an open, conversationlike feminist approach to interviewing, and how the interconnections of memory, interpretation of experience, and truth affect this study.

Overview of the Book

I begin, of course, with the couples. The partners are described at length in the first chapter. I provide detailed information about them, including the range and average age of the study participants, how long on average the couples had been together, and their educational and employment backgrounds. (All details, including class of origin, race, ethnicity, religion, and nationality are tabulated in the List of Participants at the end of the book.) I then tell the stories of four particular couples, illustrating the

Introduction

rich diversity of these intercultural relationships and introducing readers to key issues in the couple partners' lives that will be considered at length in the chapters that follow.

The second chapter illuminates how the identities of those involved in intergroup domestic partnerships are affected by living daily with someone from another cultural group. Conceiving of identity in relational terms, or as actively constructed by partners in a couple relationship within their social environment, I consider the contexts within which the partners resist and accommodate to pressures and interests acting on them to identify with particular groups and heritages. I examine how the participants come to recognize differences between themselves and their partners, how these perceived differences have affected their identities, and how they negotiate and reinvent their identities under varying social circumstances.

In chapters three and four, I explore differences that matter most to the couples inside their relationships as well as those that are salient across relations with others. Although both social class and gender are recognized by the majority of the couples as the most important differences within their relationships, and both are often linked by the partners to ethnicity or culture, class difference is a significantly more salient issue within the partnerships than is gender. On the other hand, the categories of difference most significant for persons outside the couple relationships (family members, acquaintances, strangers)—race and religion—turn out to matter significantly less to the partners inside the couple. When dealing with the outside world, however, interracial couples often encounter racism and discrimination, while those in interfaith partnerships experience pressure or even rejection from family members. Additionally, interracial same-sex couples are affected profoundly by the intersection of racism and homophobia. Nonetheless, the interracial and interfaith couples in this study are able to deal effectively with negative outside reactions and remain committed to and highly satisfied with their relationships.

Strategies of accommodation are examined in chapter five. How do partners make adjustments to each other's differences and address the pressures from outside their relationships? I examine the strategies that the partners develop to manage and resolve conflict, particularly those disagreements stemming from class and cultural differences in such areas as financial issues and family relations. Also of interest are gender differences in communication related to the development of accommodation strategies, and the shared values and commitments of the partners that allow them to transcend social group boundaries.

In the concluding chapter, I summarize the major findings of this study and then explore the implications for intercultural understanding and accommodation more generally. Positing a link between interpersonal and structural levels of social behavior and interaction, I argue that the study of achievement of cross-cultural understanding within couple partnerships offers insights to how successful accommodations may occur between different (potentially hostile and unequal) groups. Effective conflict resolution between groups may take place when each of the parties recognizes the boundaries between that which is and is not negotiable, what each group can retain, and what each needs to relinquish. As the United States becomes increasingly multicultural, conceiving of how differences can be negotiated and accommodated without loss and assimilation is crucial. This study of intercultural couples has a great deal to contribute to the understanding of that process.

1

The Couples

> We came into this [relationship] knowing full well that because of the very different ways we grew up, our different cultures, it was important for us to really pay attention to each other's perspectives. Then . . . we discovered that we had much more in common than we imagined. But still, sometimes we clash, and when that happens we take the time to discuss it. And also, the longer we are together, the better we know each other's cultures and the easier it is to understand why she does or says things that I may not agree with.
> —Banu (Asian-Indian American woman living with a Mexican American woman)

Thirty-five couples were interviewed for this study of intercultural domestic partnerships. A most interesting and enjoyable aspect of the interviews was the range of experiences, backgrounds, and personalities the couple partners revealed in the course of our conversations. The study participants come from twenty-five different nations besides the United States: Algeria, Brazil, Burma, Canada, Chile, Dominican Republic, El Salvador, England, France, Germany, Ghana, Honduras, Hungary, India, Iran, Lebanon, the Netherlands, Norway, Pakistan, Peru, the Philippines, Russia, South Africa, Switzerland, and Tanzania. Fourteen different U.S. ethnic groups are represented in the sample as well as the broad U.S. "racial" groups: Black, Hispanic/Latino/a, Asian/Pacific Islander,

Native American, and White. The partners sometimes met in unlikely places far from their homes of origin, only to discover that they had much in common with the "other" who at first appeared inscrutable. Sometimes, the partners' initial shared interests and understandings gave way, over time, to discovery of deep-seated cultural differences that emerged as the couples' circumstances changed.

As might be expected of such a diverse sample, the personalities of the participants span a wide range from extroverted and highly animated to reticent and surly. While each couple is different and has unique stories to tell, common patterns became noticeable after several interviews. A striking commonality among these otherwise very disparate couples is that almost all make a distinction between differences that are meaningful inside their relationships as opposed to those that matter to people outside the couple—a focus of two key chapters of this book.

The majority (thirty-two) of the couples in this study are heterosexual and six are same-sex partnerships. Twenty-four, or 63 percent, are international relationships in which one of the partners was born and raised in a country other than the United States. Twenty-two (58 percent) of the couples are interracial, twenty-seven (70 percent) are interreligious, and twenty-one (55 percent) have partners from different social class backgrounds. It is obvious from this breakdown that many of the couples possess several dimensions of difference simultaneously. Although they were selected on the basis of having at least two social characteristics that varied between them, the majority of the couples in the sample (66 percent) hold at least three. Thus many couples are simultaneously international, interracial, interfaith, and/or interclass.

The participants range in age from twenty-six to eighty years; the average age for the sample is forty-four years. The partners tend to be close in age; the modal (most frequent) age difference for the couples is two years. The biggest age difference between partners is fourteen years and the smallest is one year.

The average length of living together as a couple for all the unions is twelve years, ranging from two to thirty-six years. This suggests considerable stability for the relationships given that the median length of marriage in the United States in 2000 was seven and one-half years (U.S. Census Bureau 2008a). The couple partners knew each other on average two and one-half years before they either decided to marry or to make a commitment to stay together. This supports other studies that, contrary to conventional thought, have found that intergroup couples invest a considerable amount of time into their relationships before committing to long-term unions (Bratter and King 2008; Diggs 2001; McNamara, Tempenis, and Walton 1999).

There is significant variation among the study participants in education and occupations. Some have only a high school education, others hold college degrees, and some have attained advanced degrees. Within couples, the partners generally have similar levels of education, although in six cases one partner has considerably more education than the other. The jobs held by the participants range from being self-employed in a small business to college professor, journalist, high school or middle school teacher, restaurant server, or store clerk. Most couple partners' occupations tend to be similar;[1] however, in seven cases (18 percent) one of the partners has a white-collar or professional occupation (e.g., teacher or counselor) and the other a working-class occupation (e.g., clerk or construction worker). Women are homemakers in 22 percent of the heterosexual couples.

During the interviews, participants were asked whether their experiences predisposed them to be more open to a relationship with someone from another cultural, national, racial, or religious group.[2] Their responses run contrary to expectations that such individuals invariably would have traveled widely or were exposed in other sustained ways to those outside their own cultures and groups. Although some of the participants had traveled abroad considerably or lived in multicultural environments in the United States, most (60 percent) grew up in homogeneous neighborhoods or communities and had limited exposure to other ethnic, racial, national, or religious groups until they met their partners. Indeed, it was through their intercultural unions that most came to appreciate such differences.

Four Couples

To illustrate the range of variation and commonality of couples in the sample, let's look at four partnerships in detail. The accounts and histories of the four couples should orient the reader to the issues facing intercultural domestic partnerships that will be explored in greater depth in the chapters that follow.

The four couples profiled exemplify the multiple ways in which categories of social difference between the partners (gender, race, ethnicity, nationality, class, religion, and sexuality) can combine to affect the partners and their relationships with others. These cases also illustrate how the couples address and negotiate those differences they perceive as significant in their relationships. Although some differences are problematic and sometimes even painful for the couples, coming from different social and cultural backgrounds is highly appreciated by the partners and perceived as mostly positive aspects of their unions.

Sheila and Gabriel

Sheila, a slender and lively fifty-year-old African American woman, has been married twenty-six years to fifty-one-year old Gabriel, a heavyset, soft-spoken black African. At the time of their interviews the couple had two children, both female, in college. Sheila is employed as a director of human resources for a large corporation, while Gabriel is the vice president of operations for a medium-size electronics business firm. Their combined income allows them to live comfortably in a large suburban home in an east coast city.

Sheila is one of three children born and raised by her mother in a poor neighborhood of a U.S. metropolis. Sheila's father died when she was very young, leaving her mother to raise the children by herself with occasional help from extended family members. Gabriel was born and lived the first twenty years of his life in Ghana. He is an only child whose father also died when he was an infant, and his mother never remarried. Gabriel's family was financially well off, owning a great deal of farmland and real estate property. Sheila's family went to a Baptist church during her childhood and Gabriel was brought up Catholic; however, he later became a Methodist, while Sheila remained spiritual but not attached to any particular religious denomination. At the time of their interviews the partners were members of a Baptist church.

After getting his undergraduate degree in England, Gabriel came to study business administration in the United States. He and Sheila met on a blind date while they were both graduate students and she was working on a master's degree in human resources. As Sheila explains,

> My roommate called and set us up. [She said] "I have a guy for you to meet." I said okay. And then I called her back, and I said, "You know, I really don't know about this blind date.... I think I'm gonna cancel. So we cancelled. And this is my best friend. She called me back. She said, [Sheila] can you please see this guy? I think you're really gonna like him. I said, "Okay, just to please you." We got engaged two months to the day after we met, and we got married two months after our engagement.

The short period of time from the first meeting until they made a commitment is very unusual for participants of this study. Yet this couple took their time when it came to another important life-altering decision—they waited seven years to have their first child (wanting first to finish graduate school and become established in their jobs). A few years later, Sheila and Gabriel decided to move to Ghana; after ten years, they returned to live permanently in the United States.

The partners' awareness of significant cultural differences between them was immediate, particularly on Sheila's part. From the beginning, she was conscious of the fact that Gabriel, although of the same race, was from a different nationality and culture, and that this difference carried a host of implications for their future together.

> That was my biggest fear, ... telling my family about this man, because I knew that I'd have to leave the United States.... [Gabe] is an only child and he had an elderly mother. He had to go back, ... that was something we knew had to happen.... How would my mother like that? .... She raised her kids by herself, and her oldest child's going, not to another state, but to another continent.... I was not sure I could live comfortably in his culture ... because it was so different from how I was raised and lived my life.

Sheila's mother and siblings, however, liked Gabriel instantly and warmly welcomed him into the family after the couple married. Sheila's mother, devastated when the couple left to live in Ghana, made Gabriel promise that he would make it possible for Sheila to come back home at least once a year, a promise he kept despite the heavy financial burden of travel.

While in Ghana, Sheila and Gabriel were both employed full time in the same business firm. Her employment outside the home unfortunately caused a great deal of friction between the couple and Gabriel's mother and extended family, who believed that a wife's place was in the home raising children. As Sheila recalls,

> His mother felt and some of his aunts . . . thought that my being a career woman was just not the proper thing. . . , that my primary responsibility should be to my home and children, that a career and a profession was not important. That was an expectation that his family had of me. . . . And that was never a problem for us here [in the United States].

Very supportive of his partner's career, Gabriel mediated between Sheila and his family. When his relatives criticized Sheila for not being home enough or not entertaining the family as was considered proper for a wife, he would step in and explain that she had gotten an education in order to work and that he and Sheila were in agreement about this. Because he took Sheila's side, Gabriel's family was not able to divide the couple.

The couple, who had two young daughters while they were in Ghana, was pressured by Gabriel's extended family to have a son. As Gabriel explains,

> A cultural problem that existed . . . was the insistence by my family that we have a son. It was difficult for my people to understand that [Sheila] and I decided to have only two children, and since none was male we were not going to try to have more. In my culture it is believed that a woman who does not bear a son does not love her husband. They forget that it is the man and the woman who make babies.

Gabriel, as Sheila notes, is unlike many of the men she met in Ghana who expect their wives to adhere to traditional gender norms. He supports Sheila's professional goals, shares with her the household chores, and the couple together makes all major decisions affecting the family.

After Gabriel's mother died, the couple decided to return to the United States to be closer to Sheila's now aging mother and to provide better educational opportunities for their children. Although the pressures from outsiders in Ghana were no longer a problem, differences within the couple surfaced due to new circumstances.

One such cultural difference became the partners' very different approaches to raising their children. In Ghana, their two daughters had been raised largely by a nanny who took care of the girls while the parents were working. Upon returning to the States, the couple could no longer afford a caretaker for the children and had to take on more responsibility for their daily care and upbringing. The partners soon ran up against their quite divergent views and practices on childrearing. As Gabriel admits,

> We didn't have a lot of disagreement [about the children] until we came back to the United States. We were all okay with the kids being disciplined [by their nanny and extended family]. But when we came here we really had a difference in the way we saw things regarding the kids. The other children were doing things and I didn't want them to do it because other kids were doing it, but [Sheila] would say, "Oh, it's okay." I'd say, "Oh, no, these are our kids. They can be different."

Sheila also is aware of this divide.

> We have very different views of raising children and that's the biggest problem that we have in our marriage. My husband has a philosophy that children should be seen and not heard. It's part of the African tradition. . . . A lot of that comes from the fact that we bring to parenthood all our childhood experiences. In coming out of a culture where parents and children have very separate domains that don't cross over, you don't even know how to cross over if you wanted to. . . . I'm an American—just the opposite. . . . I figure you have to be a friend to your kids as well as a parent. . . . I want them to be able to come to me with their problems and they can do that with me. If they've got a problem, they don't go tell him. They go to tell mom first because she's always open.

Sheila sees Gabriel's strict disciplinary approach and the emotional and physical distance between him and their daughters as related to a Ghanaian cultural gender norm that a father should not be too close to his daughters. "In [Ghana], the men—you don't touch your daughter!

I don't know at what age he stopped hugging, touching the girls. He told me, 'I can't do that because they're girls, and it might be taken the wrong way.'"

As a consequence of this cultural difference, Sheila became quite close to her daughters, while Gabriel assumed the role of a distant father figure. This pattern was abruptly interrupted, however, when the younger daughter, upon leaving for college, confronted Gabriel about what she perceived as his lack of involvement in her life. According to Sheila, the daughter loudly proclaimed: "Dad, you don't know me! You never talk to me. You don't know who my friends are. You don't know anything about me! You don't know me as a person." Sheila feared that Gabriel would "write [the daughter] off" and never speak to her again after the outburst—that would have been the culturally expected response in Ghana—but instead he started visiting both daughters in their respective colleges and spending more time with them.

Another problem the couple recognized upon their return to the United States was different attitudes regarding financial matters. While in Africa, the partners' combined income and additional family wealth were more than sufficient to meet their needs; moreover, they generally spent less because the cultural environment did not valorize consumption. In the States, incomes did not stretch as far as they did in Ghana, their children's economic needs were changing as the girls got older, and the temptations of a consumption society beckoned. Gabriel responded by being frugal and saving as much as possible, while Sheila took advantage of the ever-present shopping mall sales. Sheila confesses, "He feels I spend too much money.... He wants to work and put everything in the bank. And I think you've got to enjoy the money.... That's what I'm working for—to enjoy life."

Such divergent views may stem from the partners' differing economic situations while they were growing up. During her interview, Sheila mentioned several times that she wants to "compensate for those early years of having to watch every cent" as her mother struggled to make ends meet. Gabriel on the other hand was brought up in a privileged situation, but one in which members of the extended family made frequent economic demands on his mother after his father's death. He learned early the value of holding on to money, which gave him an education abroad. For this couple, the economic class of origin plays an important role in influencing the partners' respective attitudes toward finances.

Despite potentially serious difficulties, Sheila and Gabriel have managed to resolve divisive issues and to maintain a satisfactory partnership. From the beginning, the partners anticipated possible problems that might stem from cultural differences and agreed how to deal with them before they came up. As Gabriel remembers,

> Even before we got married we discussed, understood, and agreed upon issues that could cause problems. For example, in my culture families and friends do not have to give you advance notice before visiting you. I explained this to [Sheila] so she would know and there'd be no surprises when my people showed up unannounced. . . . She went along with it, and our houses in [Ghana] and America have always been opened to people. . . . As a male I am expected to provide help to family members who need it. This includes extended family. And it is expected that family members will assist us in raising our children, especially in the early years. Before we went together to Africa, [Sheila] knew about all of this and we didn't have problems.

Problems that the couple was not prepared in advance to deal with, especially childrearing and finances, were not easy to address. After their return from Ghana, Sheila became troubled by how distant Gabriel had become from their daughters and she increasingly resented being told that she should not spend her own money on clothes or other items. On the other hand, Gabriel was frustrated by Sheila's spending habits and unaware of the extent of the alienation from his children until the younger daughter confronted him.

Over time, the partners have learned how to resolve the issues that threaten their marriage. As Sheila explains,

> We had a lot of unfinished business, things that we didn't resolve. And . . . [so] something will happen and then it all explodes up into a big fight. We've gotten better over the years, particularly over the last couple of years, . . . through my mother, who has said to me that if he doesn't talk,

you will have to be the one to reason.... Sometimes you're in a painful situation, you say let's not talk about it, it'll go away. And we've done that for years. It'll go away. But it doesn't. Three months later it will resurface. So I've gotten better at addressing the painful [things].... I know what the basic source of our difficulties are—they're money and children. So I do try to cut back [on spending] now, more than I did before, trying to make him happy. So we're working on that. Before I make any major purchases, I discuss it with him, which I used not to do. I'd just go out and spend a couple hundred dollars—because I feel I work, I'm entitled to spend money as I wish. He says we should talk about it. I say, okay, he has a good point.

Gabriel and Sheila today more frequently discuss their divergent approaches to the children, which helps each to understand better the other's assumptions and practices. Sheila realizes that it was not just Gabriel's cultural upbringing that was responsible for his standoffishness with his daughters, but that she also unconsciously "took away" from him the raising of the children.

In African cultures or societies, if the marriage dissolves the children go with the father, . . . the father has first custody rights. I lived in[Ghana] where marriages dissolved and the husbands took the children. So, deep down, I always had the fear that if we ever broke up, he would take the girls. So that's why—I realize now—I always kept them very close to me.... And I can't tell him that. I did tell him I was sorry for what I did by pulling them away, but I never told him the reason why.

Sheila's painful revelation and her decision not to tell her partner about it weigh heavily on her. She seems to have drawn a line as to how far she can be open with Gabriel without hurting him and she stops short of letting him know her deepest fear. Nonetheless, Sheila feels that she and Gabriel are working successfully on the issues with their children, that Gabriel's relationships with his daughters have improved greatly, and that, as a result, their partnership has reached a new level of understanding. Gabriel also believes that the marriage is now stronger due to better communication.

> Something I learned from [Sheila] over the years was to resolve our conflicts and disagreements before going to bed. I realized that it was important that we talk about any problem. . . . What has made it easier for us over the years is that we are now both able to admit when we are wrong and to say that we are sorry.

At the time of their interviews, after living together for twenty-six years, the couple recognized clearly the benefits of an intercultural partnership. Sheila saw that her marriage to Gabriel enriched her as a person.

> The cultural piece is a whole new dimension and a whole new layer because you always have to interpret things in terms of respecting the cultural background that [your partner] comes from. You don't want to offend him. There's always that layer of interpretation, . . . and it's created a greater sensitivity because I always have to read him—he can't say to me, you know, it's a cultural thing. I've got to be able to assimilate that and come to that conclusion. There's . . . insight and introspection that you develop—you've always got to look a little deeper for things.

Gabriel likewise recognized a far-reaching change in him as a result of the relationship.

> Like many of her people [African Americans], she is very forthright. In my culture, we're rather indirect and it is acceptable to tell "white lies". . . . She has taught me to be more open and direct in addressing issues and to talk about any problems we may have.

Overall, the couple reports that they are "in a very good place right now" (Sheila) and acknowledge "similar attitudes about life and the important things" (Gabriel). At last contact, four years after the interviews, the partners were celebrating their thirtieth wedding anniversary.

Suzy and Russell

A second-generation Japanese American, twenty-nine-year-old Suzy and her thirty-one-year-old Polish American (also second generation) spouse, Russell, live in a spacious, three-bedroom house in an older, ethnically diverse neighborhood of a midwestern city. Suzy is a petite and reflective woman with an open, engaging smile, while Russell's large but trim frame is matched by a congenial and outgoing personality. At the time of their interviews, the partners were expecting their first child.

On maternity leave from her job, Suzy works as a dental hygienist, and Russell is self-employed in a small business. Suzy is a follower of Buddhism, which she regards more as a "philosophy of life" than a religion; Russell, who grew up Catholic, stopped going to church in his teens and is not religious today. When I interviewed them, the partners had been married for seven years but had known each other for two years before marrying. They met in a west coast city when Russell came to Suzy's place of work for a dental appointment and she cleaned his teeth.

Suzy and Russell took their time getting to know each other. Both admit that the different racial (Asian and Caucasian) and ethnic (Japanese and Polish) backgrounds made them mutually cautious about getting involved. Neither had previously dated a person from another "racial" group and Suzy especially was concerned about "getting involved with someone who wouldn't understand my culture." Russell for his part admits that the physical dimension of the difference was very alluring.

> She did look different than the women I had been attracted to in the past. When I first saw her, I thought she was so beautiful, so exotic looking. . . . I was conscious of her sexuality, she seemed like a rare flower, . . . like an exotic orchid.

It took Russell and Suzy six months to start dating and another six before they became intimate and declared feelings of love. The partners' families accepted the intercultural relationship. The marriage was a civil ceremony at city hall with aspects of both cultures showcased in the reception afterwards: "We had both Japanese and Polish food. . . . [Russell's] family and friends sang appropriate Polish songs. And [Suzy] put on a kimono for the occasion."

The couple was initially most keenly aware of differences revolving around food and lifestyle. As Suzy explains,

> We liked different foods—he wouldn't touch sushi and other Japanese foods I liked to cook and I didn't like the meat and potatoes meals he was used to. He missed his family and the Polish community where he used to live, and I missed my family, too. [Russell's] family and friends often had big parties with lots of drinking and singing, and I wasn't used to that kind of partying. He wanted us to have parties and invite the neighbors and people we worked with, but I didn't feel comfortable with these people. And I'm not a big sports fan . . . because we never watched sports back home, and [he and] his family were really into that. We seemed to have very little in common at first.

When Russell was offered a new job, the couple decided to move to the Midwest. Russell notes, "We were on our own [at that point] and had to come to terms with our cultural differences." That divide seemed exacerbated by the new environment in which they lived. According to Suzy,

> When we moved, we were able [to afford] to buy a little house in [a suburban town of a midwestern city] and it's a very white and conservative place. We were the only mixed couple there as far as we knew. Our neighbors weren't very friendly, they were always watching us, and we felt like we were really different. The first three years that we lived in [the suburb] we constantly had misunderstandings and disagreements because we thought we were so different.

Over time, the couple found ways to address the differences that were increasingly problematic. As Russell explains,

> We adjusted. . . . We sort of looked for a third way, something in between our two cultures. Often we'd find things from the mainstream American culture that we could both relate to, like eating pizza and going to the movies. Now we have some Japanese and Polish friends and also some from other cultures, and that helps . . . us be more ourselves and not to be so defensive about our cultures.

Suzy and Russell were eventually able to afford to buy a house within the city in an older, lower-middle-class, ethnically diverse neighborhood. Moving away from a homogeneous, white suburb and into this community made it possible for them to live among people from a variety of races and cultures, including other intercultural couples. Suzy recognizes that this new environment helped the couple deal with their own cultural differences by making them seem more ordinary.

> I think we pay less attention to the differences now.... They become part of everyday life and eventually you don't even notice them.... The neighborhood where we live, there are many mixed couples, and nobody singles us out any more.

Over time, too, Russell and Suzy came to more keenly appreciate each other's cultures. As Russell acknowledges,

> We know that our cultures are different but it's okay that we're different—it's not a big deal any more.... The differences are there, but our cultures have sort of blended together more. Each of us ... has become more familiar with the other's culture and so it's not as noticeable as before. We visited Japan last year, and I sort of felt at home there. I don't really speak the language, but things were very familiar to me; it's like I was more of an insider than an outsider.... Because of my marriage I am able to have a real appreciation of another culture and to feel like I'm part of that culture in some way.

Suzy agrees.

> Because of my exposure to [Russell's] culture, I was able to see the culture I grew up in and lived [in] for most of my life a little more critically, but also to see its positive aspects.... It's really great to be able to share, with the person I love and respect most, those positive aspects and to take from his culture the things he want[s] to share with me.

The aspects of Russell's culture that Suzy finds particularly appealing include "the warmth and hospitality of his Polish community" and "some of the food and customs, especially around the big holidays." Russell eventually learned to enjoy many of the Japanese foods that Suzy considers a staple of her diet, and now is sensitive to "Japanese people's loyalty to their families, their hard work, and a kind of gentleness toward each other." This couple's "third way" of being together involves appreciating and, to some extent, incorporating into their daily existence aspects of their two cultures along with aspects of what they refer to as "American mainstream culture."

When disagreeing, both make an effort to talk through problems and issues. Suzy discloses that "We just talk. And we listen to each other and respect each other's point of view." Russell tells how the couple resolved a recent argument about when Suzy's mother would come to visit after their child was born. Suzy wanted her mother to be there at the time of the baby's birth, but Russell preferred that she come a few days later so that he would have time alone with Suzy and their child during the first few days.

> We talked about it for a long time, and she began to see my point, but then I also saw that it was really important for her to have her mother here. In the end we decided that her mother will come [in time for the birth] and [Suzy] will explain to her mother that I want to be able to spend time alone with her and the baby.

Although Suzy and Russell both came from families where "mothers took care of the house and kids, and fathers did the yard work and didn't do any cooking or cleaning," the partners do not adhere to traditional gender expectations. Suzy indicates that Russell and she "both have jobs and share the housework, too. We both cook and clean and do the shopping." Russell confirms,

> Since we both work, we divide the housework equally. We both like to cook so we take turns doing it, and sometimes we cook together. We usually clean the house on weekends and shop for groceries; . . . whoever has the time does laundry when dirty clothes pile up.

The partners attribute their egalitarian relationship to living away from their families and original ethnic communities and also to an abiding awareness as intercultural partners that they can create a life for themselves different from what they have known before. Suzy claims that had she married someone from her own culture and lived among other Japanese Americans, her marriage would have been more traditional. Pointing to family and community pressure on women to stay at home, she cites examples of "Japanese American women friends who married men from their culture and they're not employed; they stay home with the kids and their husbands support them." Russell, in a cohabiting relationship with a Polish American woman before meeting Suzy, describes the prior relationship as very traditional. His more equal partnership with Suzy is possible, he believes, because of "the freedom to take from our cultures . . . those aspects that we want, and not to accept those things we don't, and to build something new. . . . It just couldn't be a traditional relationship; it had to be a relationship between two equals."

At the time of their interviews, Suzy and Russell were highly satisfied with their marriage of seven years. The couple decided to have a child because, as Suzy says,

> We are both pretty happy about our situation now, where we are as a couple. We like where we live and we like our jobs, and together we feel strong, so we can provide a good environment for a baby.

Both partners are genuinely appreciative of and enthusiastic about being in an intercultural union, and recognize its benefits beyond their personal relationship. Russell is aware that, because of his intercultural marriage, he has become more open to other cultures; for example, he consciously hired an employee who was an Asian immigrant.

> I had several people applying for the job, and [of] the final two I interviewed, one was [a white] American and the other from [a South Asian country]. They had very similar credentials and experience but I decided to go with the [Asian] because I thought he'd bring a different cultural aspect to the business. And I was right; he's been a great employee. But I probably wouldn't have made this decision if I wasn't married to someone from a different culture.

In Russell's case, his intercultural partnership promotes understanding of the benefits of diversity in the workplace, encouraging him to seize an opportunity to diversify his business staff.

Selma and Banu

Selma, a twenty-six-year-old Mexican American woman, has been cohabiting for three years with Banu, a twenty-eight-year-old Asian-Indian American woman. Throughout her interview, Banu kept tossing back her long black hair and gesticulated animatedly with her hands as she spoke. The rather reserved Selma spoke slowly and distinctly, as if measuring every word, smiling occasionally when she paused to reflect on the questions I asked. Both were born in the United States and both have always lived in the same west coast city. Banu was raised in a middle-class Indian immigrant family; Selma, whose parents were undocumented immigrants from Mexico, grew up in poverty. Having earned a bachelor's degree in the social sciences, Selma works for a community service organization, while Banu, with a master's degree in computer science, is a programmer for a medium-size computer firm. They live in a two-bedroom apartment of a converted house in a gentrifying interracial urban neighborhood that is populated largely by Latino/a and Asian immigrants. The two met as university students and both were active in a student organization. Although Selma's family of origin is Catholic, she rejected the religion in college. Banu, raised a Muslim, considers her religion as a spiritual outlook on life rather than an institutional affiliation.

Before moving in together, the partners expected to deal with some considerable differences; they recognized they "com[e] from very different cultural backgrounds" and could "see differences right away." These apparent dissimilarities involved mainly "holidays and food" as well as "ways you're supposed to relate to different people." According to Selma,

> In [Banu's] culture you're supposed to defer to your older brother and your male relatives, but you can argue [with] and even put down your older sister and other women, . . . [though not] your mother-in-law. In my culture [Mexican American] you're supposed to defer to older women, too.

Banu points out that Selma's family was initially more welcoming of her than her own was of Selma because, "They, the Mexican Americans, tend to be more friendly toward outsiders than [are] Indians." She also didn't like that Selma dressed sometimes in "really tight tops and short skirts and bright colors . . . that to me looks kind of, well, I don't want to say 'cheap,' but that's what comes to my mind when I see women dress like that. I see a lot of Latinas dress this way."

The partners however were "surprised to find that there were some things in our backgrounds that were not that different" (Banu). As Selma relates,

> It turned out that we both came from pretty traditional types of families and neighborhoods with fathers heads of households and mothers who did everything in the house regardless if they worked or not, where people had much the same ideas about how to raise children. . . . The specific customs differed a lot, but there was that basic similarity.

Selma and Banu have been able to accommodate successfully to the cultural differences between them. When it became apparent that their culinary tastes clashed, as Selma liked "bland Tex-Mex food" and Banu enjoyed "very spicy dishes," each began using spices in moderation when cooking a meal. Over time, too, Selma has learned to appreciate Banu's hotter foods, and Banu has started enjoying some of the less spicy Mexican-American dishes. Both partners appreciate taking part in the various holiday celebrations of the families and generally get along well with each other's relatives. Once Banu explained to Selma how she felt about her choice of clothing, Selma agreed not to dress in revealing clothes when visiting Banu's family.

Although the partners initially recognized "racial" differences between them (Selma claims, "From the beginning, we were aware that she is Asian and I'm Latina"), this has not been a divisive issue in their relationship. The couple asserts that the differences they notice are cultural and that "looking different is not something that we pay attention to."

An unexpected difference that has created a problem for the partners inside the relationship is their divergent social class backgrounds. Experiencing poverty for much of the time she was growing up, particularly through childhood and into high school, Selma is very careful about conserving resources but also generously shares her income with friends and relatives in need. Banu, on the other hand, was brought up by parents who had been wealthy in India but became middle class after moving to the United States. For much of her childhood, Banu witnessed her parents struggling to "get ahead" and "never accepting that they had enough money because it was always less than what they left behind." Banu admits that

> Because most of my life I was taught that the way to get ahead is to save and to invest your money, and not to give any of it away, when I see [Selma] just giving most of what she makes not only to family but to the homeless shelter, to AIDS victims, you name it, I get upset. . . . We've been talking about buying a house, but she has no savings at all, and I don't think it's fair for me to have to come up with the whole down payment.

And Selma finds Banu's attachment to "getting ahead" irritating:

> She's a great person, very kind, caring, and generous with her time, but when it comes to money, she wants to make it grow so she can get ahead. She saves a portion of every paycheck, and then she invests the savings in mutual funds. It's often annoying to me that she doesn't want to donate money to community organizations and causes. . . . She has gotten better about it recently, but that's because of my nagging.

Although the couple has attempted to resolve this difference (Banu started to donate some money to the causes that Selma felt passionate about and Selma made a stab at saving), the partners acknowledge that, unlike other issues, this one is not resolved to their satisfaction. As Banu states,

> I'm not sure we can change our attitudes much. . . . It's the way we are and we have to accept that. We agree about most things and get along very well, but in this area, well, I don't think we can change.

And Selma confirms,

> I would like to see her be more generous with her money, but I know that . . . might be just asking too much of her. I know she tries, and I'm trying too, to be more responsible about my finances. But this is . . . one of those things we may just have to "live and let live."

Another problem that Selma and Banu were facing at the time of the interviews centered on coming out to their families as a lesbian couple. Both have come out to friends, but have been unable to do so with their families. Selma explains,

> I haven't come out to my family and [Banu] hasn't come out to hers. We did tell them that we're living together, but my parents and her parents think it's only as roommates, as friends. We didn't actually tell them that; they just assumed it.... We decided that it would be better for now [not to tell them].... They are very conservative, very traditional, and if they knew about us, I'm sure they wouldn't be able to deal with it. I've thought about this a lot; I think about it all the time. And I know that as much as my family loves me, me being a lesbian is just something that's beyond their ability to accept. They're very religious, too.

And Banu observes,

> Well, they [Banu's parents and siblings] accepted [Selma], they like her very much, ... but they don't realize really that she and I are, uhm, involved, that we're living together as a couple, rather than just friends.... They are very old fashioned, very traditional Indian, even after so many years of living in this country. They still live mostly among Indians, and keep up the customs, the holidays, and all that. So, they just couldn't deal with my being lesbian.

Selma and Banu, however, are aware that they cannot keep their sexual orientation a secret from their families indefinitely. Selma admits,

> I realize that sooner or later they'll have to find out. And my hope is that with time, they'll accept [Banu] as my partner. They actually already love her, my parents treat her like a daughter, and so as long as we keep it in the family, so that the relatives and neighbors and others don't know, I'm thinking that with time they'll accept my, our, situation.

Selma's hope is that eventually she and Banu will come out to their parents and siblings. As long as the extended family and others residing in their families' neighborhoods do not know, it will be easier for the families to accept the partners' sexual orientation. The couple fears the sanctions that the larger community might impose on their parents if their daughters' sexual orientation became known. Meanwhile, living partly closeted lives places a strain on Banu's and Selma's relations with their families of origin.

Despite the tensions created in this relationship by the social class differences and the couple's decision not to disclose their sexual orientation to their families, the partners are highly satisfied with their life together as a couple. They report sharing all the housework equally and have found an effective way to resolve arguments. Selma and Banu also appreciate deeply one another's cultures and have renewed interest in their own. Selma states,

> [Banu] is very respectful of my culture, and I am of hers. We're both interested in learning more about each other's culture, and . . . living with her has made me even more aware of my cultural roots. About a year ago, I did some reading about the history of Mexican Americans in the U.S., which I never bothered doing before. And that was because [Banu] started asking me all these questions that I couldn't answer, and I got curious, too. And she's taught me a lot about India and Indian traditions . . . from the part of India that her family's from. . . . I know now more about my own culture, and I'm proud of who I am. I think I have a firmer cultural identity than [I did] before. But at the same time, I also feel like I'm part of her culture, too, because I participate in the holidays, the rituals, the meals, that she does and I'm learning the nuances.

And Banu confirms,

> When I left home and went to college, that's probably when I was really exposed to American culture and I found myself conforming more . . . and starting to give up some [cultural] things. But when I started to live with [Selma], I actually went back to some of the cultural things I gave up before. She was always very interested in my culture and wanted to know more about it. She kind of encouraged me to cook Indian food and she asked about the music, the holidays, and so forth. . . . [S]he wanted to know and to accept aspects of my culture. And I reciprocated [by asking] about her culture; I was interested in the history of Mexican Americans, and since she didn't

know that much about it, we both started to read . . . and to discuss . . . [what we learned.] I also wanted to learn from her about Mexican American customs. . . . I think I have become a more open-minded person. I am able to be more accepting of people from other cultures, especially Mexican Americans.

Both partners recognize and value highly the benefits of being in an intercultural relationship.

Patsy and Don

Patsy is a forty-six-year-old Asian woman, born and raised in the Philippines, married to Don, an African American man three years her senior. Patsy is slender, of medium height with shoulder-length black hair and lively hazel eyes, while Don is considerably taller than his spouse, trim, with expressive, deep-set brown eyes; both are outgoing and talkative.

Raised in a middle-class family in a large Philippine city, Patsy had the opportunity to attend a university where she studied English and American literature. Don came from a working-class family and lived until he left for college in a predominantly black community of a large east coast U.S. city. The partners met in the Philippines when Don was working in a refugee resettlement program and Patsy was teaching ESL (English as second language) to Southeast Asians who participated in that program. They dated for several months and were married by a judge in a city hall civil ceremony. The couple lived in the Philippines for eight years and then moved to the United States after Don lost his job and could not find another one in the Philippines. At the time of their interviews, the partners had been married fourteen years and had four children. Patsy is a server in a restaurant and Don is a counselor in a state hospital. They live in a modest house in a suburb of a major U.S. east coast city.

Patsy's loss of occupational status upon moving to the United States weighs heavily on her. In her interview, she talks at length about this unfavorable change.

> The work I'm doing here is blue collar. I don't even tell the people there, back home [what I do]. . . . I used to study and teach in the Philippines [in a master's program] and now I have no career here. . . . I would really like to

The Couples

> teach.... I asked to sub at the school where my children go, but I was never called.... I [wanted] to be an ESL teacher but because I was very new and I had no certification [it did not work out].

Patsy found out that obtaining ESL certification included going back to college, which she could not afford. She thus found a job serving in a restaurant that is "just a minute from the house." In order to obtain a little more income, in the evenings and on weekends she also provides care for an elderly woman who lives down the street. Patsy views living in the United States and performing these jobs as a sacrifice that she is making so that Don can be employed and that her "children can have the best education possible ... and have access to a modern life ... that's what gives me meaning." However, Don reports that she often feels undervalued and isolated, and periodically becomes depressed.

Throughout their interviews, Patsy and Don talked a great deal about their experiences in an interracial marriage. Initially, they were very much aware of the race difference between them (perceived mainly as physical features, especially skin color). When Don first asked Patsy to go out with him, she refused, recognizing Don's race as problematic for her.

> PATSY: [Don] being a black man ... I really didn't want to mess around with him.... I was always friendly to foreigners, but not a black man! ... I would have smashed my reputation [by going out] with a black man.... It would have been the same as [being] a prostitute ... we might have been misconstrued as having sex together.... I did not want to be identified with a black man.... In my country, ... a very colonialistic country, ... white is beautiful and ... black people ... are the pygmies, the aborigines, and they are always considered so [much] less [than white people].

Don talks about being aware of the stereotype of "the Westerner wan[ting] an Oriental ... and then on the other hand, the African American stereotyped male [being] more virile and all that." However, he claims that Patsy being Asian was not an initial barrier for him because he had been around people of different races since childhood. "My mother's best friend was white and we were very close to her. I've always been ...

[39]

kind of predisposed to people that are different. And I never really thought much about it."

Don was persistent and eventually Patsy agreed to a date as long as they were chaperoned. Over time, as the partners became better acquainted, Patsy realized that Don was "so nice and educated . . . he had all these credentials . . . all this scholastic background, and it impressed me . . . [getting to know him] erased this misconception" she had of blacks. Don also appreciated Patsy's educational background: "She was mature . . . she was very intellectual . . . and that's how we got together and we enjoyed that."

Nevertheless, each of the partners experienced racism from persons outside their relationship. While the couple lived in the Philippines, Patsy was often the target of insulting questions about her marriage to Don from family members and acquaintances.

> PATSY: And people would ask me, "You are very light skinned and why did you ever marry an American? A Negro? And as black as coal! Is he the only last American? . . . Or they would ask me terrible questions like, does he have a big stick dick? Or they would even take my son's shirt off and look [at] how big is his rear.

Don also encountered racial discrimination at work, and later when he and Patsy ran a small business he was often exploited by Patsy's relatives and acquaintances, who assumed he was an easy target and took financial advantage of him. Patsy, who "had connections and . . . would just drop names," was able to keep her marriage and family in "good standing" in the community despite widespread disapproval expressed by her extended family and community members.

When the couple moved to the United States, it was Patsy's turn to experience discrimination. Don recalls Patsy trying to be active in their church, "working with other people, and feeling that these people don't recognize [her contributions] or [that] they put her down . . . because she's Asian, . . . and that's been very distressing to her." In her interview, Patsy remarks several times that she finds some Americans to be "nasty and negative" and that she's had to learn to deal with "people tell[ing] you something that is totally outrageous, that's a projection of their own prejudices." She also has realized that she and her family are considered black in the community where they reside: "Where we live, [we're] the only non-white [family], I'm the only non-American. So we feel black there." Moreover, Patsy discovered that, as in the Philippines, in the United States Don is often perceived negatively by people simply because he happens to be a black man.

> PATSY: When we were very new there [the first place they lived in the United States] we asked for some food from the food pantry [from the church they joined] but the person who was assigned to handle the food . . . made a comment that Blacks might have a criminal record. She said, "Every walking black man here is a criminal anyway." And what can he do about his black skin? Nothing! Until he dies, he will be a criminal to some white people here.

Although race became less significant in their personal relationship over time, it continues to be the main difference recognized by those around Patsy and Don. The partners deal with incidents of racism by talking to each other about their treatment by others and not letting themselves be bothered by racist remarks or discrimination. As Don points out, "Now it's just . . . we kinda even laugh about it, and [Patsy] says, 'these Americans!' and I know she doesn't mean all of the Americans [just the ones that hurt them]."

And Patsy acknowledges,

> These nasty things that were said to me in the past . . . would jolt me before, but now I'm not so upset because [I've] gone through it . . . and I have learned to cope. . . . If that's the way they like it, fine with me. . . . I only have to live with my own conscience, and I always say to myself, "who are these people who are mean like that because of their lives?" And because [Don] and I have that kind of partnership . . . we have a good relationship . . . we are able together to deal with it [racism].

Differences that do create problems for Don and Patsy inside their couple relationship are cultural. The partners report having serious arguments throughout their marriage because they are from very different cultural backgrounds. Especially problematic for the couple are cultural expectations related to gender. For instance, Patsy, who was raised in a community and extended family where women had hired help ("maids") in the home, expected to be responsible for managing the household when she got married. However, when Don lost his job with the refugee resettlement program and the partners were struggling economically, Patsy herself did most of the housework and childcare. Don, however, who was pretty independent by the time he met Patsy, had other ideas:

> We would figuratively speaking have to come to blows if I wanted to cook my own food ... or if I wanted to wash the dishes ... she's supposed to take care of you. ... I was raised by strong women and had to learn to pull my weight ... and I'm the kind of guy I like to make my own work because I [was used to it] and enjoy it. ... And ... something so small would wind up a big issue. And it dawned on me that this was a cultural thing. ... And we still have things like that [disagreements over division of work in the home] but it's quite different now ... [we] kinda understand what's ... driving the situation.

> PATSY: It was a very hard process for the both of us. ... [I thought] I had to be the cook and raise the family ... and when we came here to the states, I ended up doing almost everything. ... The American notion that Asians are very submissive, that's a misnomer. We are not! We [Filipinas] come from a very matriarchal society. The women there are born feminists. They run the show. ... And we [she and Don] got better about it over the years, but we're still working this out [how to share housework].

Patsy thus expresses ambivalence about meeting traditional gender expectations under circumstances where economic resources no longer allow for hired help in the home, while Don who ostensibly wants to share household work more equally with his spouse understands Patsy's resistance as "cultural" and thus amenable to change.

Another cultural difference that the couple recognizes to be problematic for them is their divergent views regarding childrearing. Patsy is adamant that she needs to teach her children discipline the way she was taught by her parents and teachers in the Philippines.

> My mother raised us like a Puritan.... I was so used to hard work, and our teachers there, who are like terrors, so I'm so used to that kind of mentality and pushing yourself all the time.... I have children and I want them to have discipline, I want to be a role model for them.

Patsy adds that she is especially concerned that her children are self-disciplined, do well in school, and become successful because "they're biracial and that [can be] very difficult." She believes they need strong parental role models, "models of great integrity." Don, on the other hand, admits that he has been "laid back" regarding discipline and that this comes from how he was raised "by strong [African American] women" who were supportive and nurturing. He also indicates that over time the couple has "agreed on understanding of the goals that we would like to see [for their children]. But we don't agree a lot on the means." Thus, Patsy continues to be more of the disciplinarian, while Don takes a more lenient approach, although "that's beginning to change . . . I think that she's too soft and she might think I'm too hard, and the next week, I'm too soft and she's too hard, so it's an ongoing thing."

The partners admit that the success of their marriage is due in large part to compromises they are willing to make in yielding to some extent to one another's expectations. The strength in their marriage comes from their ability to talk openly and at length when they have culturally based disagreements as well as personal disappointments, or when they experience hurtful incidents. Each knows that the other is there with support, understanding, and empathy when the need arises.

> DON: When she feels isolated, she gets depressed. And I know what that's like, think how far away [she is from her country] . . . and I try to support her as much as I can . . . and I know the feeling that she's feeling.
>
> PATSY: When Don and I met, we had a meeting of . . . hearts. He's such a generous person, a very good-hearted person, he never backbites, he never talks back.... We have that kind of partnership now . . . a lot of mutual understanding, support; we have a good relationship.

Conclusion

As these four profiles show, the intercultural partnerships forming the basis of this study are quite diverse yet also demonstrate commonalities. They all share various dimensions of social difference that the partners negotiate with varying degrees of success; however, particular differences—of race, ethnicity, nationality, class, gender, or religion—are more or less salient in specific relationships. Partners identify and address only those social differences perceived to affect their relationship significantly.

As these profiles also suggest, and the following chapters demonstrate more explicitly, class of origin, gender, and ethnic differences contribute to contested issues that intercultural partners recognize to be most important within the couples. Race, religion, and sexuality, on the other hand, become especially significant in outside relationships, such as those with family members and acquaintances.

An important theme running through these couple narratives is that intergroup domestic partnerships are positive, albeit sometimes highly challenging and requiring a great deal of negotiation. Partners are granted access to and opportunities for an intimate understanding of the "other." By crossing into the world of a person from a different social group, each partner gains a potentially valuable perspective from which to see her/himself and to better comprehend that other world. The effects of such crossings of boundaries on identity will be explored in the following chapter.

2

Reinventing Cultural Identity in Intergroup Couple Relationships

> In the beginning, when you would have to think that the differences would be greater and more intact, I was so interested in . . . commonality and mutuality that I didn't notice, I didn't attribute problems or tensions to culture. . . . The longer she was here, . . . the more American she became, and yet, at the same time, I finally figured out that there was cultural stuff here; I became more aware of differences.
> —Robert (Anglo-American man married to a Russian woman)

The fact that two people living today in the United States are able to form a lasting partnership, even when they possess common social characteristics, is a remarkable feat, given high divorce rates and pressures against long-term relationships. At some level, every domestic partnership is "intercultural" as each couple develops its own unique culture out of two (Grearson and Smith 1995, xvii). In heterosexual relationships, women and men typically view their marriages in dissimilar ways (Bernard 1972; Coontz 2008; Rubin 1995). Every person comes into an intimate partnership with a different set of personal and social experiences that require some adjustment and accommodation to the other. Intercultural couples, however, in addition to situational and personality (and in heterosexual relationships sex/gender) differences, also wrestle with ethnicity, race, class, religion, and nationality—factors that provide extra substance for potential conflict and negotiation.

One consequence of domestic partnerships is identity transformation. Such change comes in part from the merging of individual persons into a new "couple," but also from at least a partial acceptance of each other's point of view, perspective, or voice. Intercultural couples confront a more complex dynamic—not only a meeting of two unique individuals, but also of two carriers of seemingly distinct cultural expectations and understandings. Such differences are especially salient when the partners are from groups perceived to be of "two different worlds," such as dissimilar countries, racial and ethnic groups, religions, and/or socioeconomic backgrounds. As I will show in this chapter, the act of crossing cultures, especially becoming intimately involved with a person from another cultural group (including nationality, race, class, and religion), typically involves the recognition of at least some difference. One's own cultural identity often becomes more salient when confronted with that of the "other."

When a person establishes a couple relationship with someone from another cultural group, does she or he continue to identify with her/his group(s) of origin or with the group(s) of her/his partner? In the past, many marriage and family sociologists assumed that if a member of a "minority" or subordinate group married a member of the "majority" or dominant group, that person's cultural identity was automatically obliterated, "assimilated" into the majority (e.g., Alba 1986; Barron 1972; Gordon 1964; Lyman and Douglas 1973). More recent research, however, has demonstrated that cultural assimilation through marriage is not automatic (Diggs 2001; Grearson and Smith 2001; Judd 1990; McCarthy 2007; Rosenblatt, Karis, and Powell 1995; Vosburgh and Juliani 1990). Not all intergroup unions are of the majority-minority type; in the United States, people are increasingly establishing domestic partnerships across minority groups and are seeking ways to hold onto their respective cultures (Clemetson 2000; Coonz 2008; Gaines 1995; Root 2001; Yancey and Lewis 2009). Moreover, assimilation into the majority culture is a complex process, depending on many factors including external pressures on intercultural couples and the choices made by the individual members of the dyads (Hutter 1990; Spickard 1989, 369–72). Cultural identity can be used in strategic ways to emphasize difference that, on the one hand, has served to create distinct oppressed minority groups but whose members, on the other hand, deploy that difference to challenge negative representations (Bernstein 2005). In this chapter, I consider the social contexts within which participants in intercultural domestic partnerships both resist and yield to pressures and interests acting on them to identify with particular groups and social heritages.

As will be seen, over time most of the participating couples became less concerned with cultural differences between the partners and their identities assumed an increasingly "hybrid" character. The perceived crossing of boundaries between cultures can be understood as part of the formation of *relational identities* or self-conceptions derived from a relationship in which the individuals are in a committed partnership. A relational identity is constructed actively by intercultural partners and is the product of two individuals and the social environments in which they are embedded (Gaines and Liu 2000, 99). Conceptualizing identities in relational terms allows the flexibility of seeing them as multiple group affiliations, as fluid and situationally contingent, at the same time as holding a degree of permanence (Ahmed 2000; Hall and du Gay 1996; Hurtado 1997, 316–17).

In the following pages, I consider how one's cultural identity is affected over time through daily coexistence with a person perceived to be from another culture. How do partners in intercultural relationships recognize differences between them? In which ways do these perceived differences affect their identities? Finally, how do couples negotiate and reinvent their identities under varying social circumstances?

The Debate Over Identity

But what is identity? In the last several decades, a rich academic discussion has flourished around the concept. Although most scholars would likely agree with the definition that one's identity comprises the meanings that she/he acquires through social interaction and thus is crucial to an understanding of an individual's sense of self (see, e.g., Howard 2000; McCall and Simmons 1996; Stephan 1992; Stryker 1980), there has been much debate regarding the *stability* of identity. Moreover, research on identity has shifted since the 1970s from an emphasis on how interpersonal interactions affect an individual's sense of self to a focus on collective identities "with gender/sexuality, race/ethnicity, and class forming the 'holy trinity' of the discursive field" (Cerulo 1997, 386). Identity research and scholarship increasingly recognizes the importance of identification processes (Ahmed 2000; Cerulo 1997; Howard 2000) and how individuals understand their identities in relation to social movements and identity politics (Bernstein 2005).

The study of collective and individual identity has moved from an earlier approach emphasizing the similarities or shared attributes that characterize a group and are internalized by its members (essentialist perspective) to social constructionism, which views identity as "an entity molded, refabricated, and mobilized in accord with reigning scripts and centers of power" (Cerulo 1997, 387), to postmodern perspectives that broaden the constructivist agenda by examining the "real, present day political and other reasons why essentialist identities continue to be invoked and often deeply felt" (Calhoun 1995, 199). Although a comprehensive summary and interrogation of these approaches is beyond the scope of this book, I will briefly discuss their contributions to understanding cultural identity.

A traditional approach to the study of identity, developed by social psychologists and sociologists, assumes that the individual self consists of various identities and trait characteristics. Although traits (sometimes also called aspects of personal identity, e.g., being shy, intelligent, aggressive, etc.) are presumed to be relatively stable over a person's life (Hurtado 1997, 309), identity characteristics may vary according to roles the individual takes on and sheds as well as specific groups with which the person associates closely or wants to join. In this view, cultural identity is acquired through identification with those groups individuals find subjectively meaningful (Elkin 1983; Howard 2000; Tajfel 1981). Even though, for instance, the ethnic identity of a particular person can change from one time to another, cultural identities are thought to derive from "a feeling of consciousness of kind that begins with commonalities of culture" (Stephan 1992, 51). Thus, at the specific time that a given person possesses a particular cultural identity, that identity is said to be comprised of recognizable and stable components (e.g., cultural values or structural location) shared by a specific cultural grouping. In this view, cultures are distinct and unitary. Such an essentialist perspective presumes that those living in multicultural settings or those of mixed cultural heritage will experience instability, conflict, and greater subjectivity of cultural identity than persons of a single ethnic heritage (McDermott and Fukunaga 1977; Piskacek and Golub 1973).

Social constructionists take issue with any categorization that establishes essential or core features of identity as distinct properties of a group's members. All categories of difference that form the basis of one's social identity (gender, race, ethnicity, class, age, nationality, (dis)ability, etc.) are conceptualized by constructionists as an ongoing project, performed and accomplished through the exchange of language and symbols (Bem 1993; Connell 1995; Taylor and Whittier 1992). Cultural identity is not anchored in ethnic or national social structures, but rather in symbolic (Alba 1990) or imagined communities (Anderson 1991) to which individuals cling as these are created and remade by social actors (Gillis 1994; Griswold 1992; Spillman 1997).

Postmodern feminist and cultural studies scholars, although supporting the antiessentialism that fuels constructionism, go even further by emphasizing variation not only across categories of difference (e.g., Asian American middle-class lesbian woman; white Anglo-Saxon working-class heterosexual man) but also within identity categories (e.g., multiple variations of "woman" and "man"). Postmodernists deconstruct and transform the concept of identity (collective and personal) from an integrated, unified entity and a socially constructed self rooted in symbolic community to one that is "fragmented and fractured, never singular but multiply constructed across different, often intersecting and antagonistic, discourses, practices and positions" (Hall 1996, 4). The self is multidimensional and shifting, composed of many, often contradictory, traits and identities that are situationally activated (Allen 1998). Identity is sometimes described as a practice rather than a category—a distinctive move away from essentialist categories such as gender or race, and as an actively constructed performance rather than preexisting roles (Bucholtz, Liang, and Sutton 1999; Butler 1993; 1998). Rather than conceiving of culture as a seamless whole or as a "package" (Narayan 2000), it is viewed by postmodernists as "a multiple and contradictory space in which differences are internal and constitutive" (Ahmed 2000, 115). Culture becomes "a resource, usually full of internal contradictions, which is used selectively by different social agents . . . within specific power relations and political discourse in and outside the collectivity" (Yuval-Davis 1997, 43). From this perspective, multiple and shifting forms of gender, class, race, sexuality, stage in life, and ability affect access to cultural resources and differentially shape individual identities.

The conception of cultural identity as fluid and situationally activated appears well suited to contemporary times, when processes of globalization disrupt most populations and cultures, and immigration (both forced and voluntary) affects people all over the world. Owing in part to such disruptions, cultural identities can no longer be embedded in historical pasts, whether material or imaginary, with which they are assumed to correspond, but rather can be more aptly understood as attempts to use "the resources of history, language, and culture in the process of becoming rather than being" (Hall 1996, 4). Thus, people who *cross* cultures, as when they move permanently to another country or establish personal relationships with those of different social backgrounds, are called upon to reinvent their identities. Persons who have lived in more than one culture or who straddle two or more cultures are "hybrids" who create "counter-narratives" that both evoke and erase cultural boundaries (Bhabha 1994). Some feminist scholars, most notably Gloria Anzaldua (1987) and those who have followed in her footsteps (see, for example, Lugones 2005; McMaster 2005; Ortega 2005), advocate "borderland identities" as products of interrelations between cultures and the blurring of boundaries between them, consciously and subjectively constructed by participants.

A notion of cultural identity that applies most readily to the reality of the couples included in this study resides somewhere between the essentialist and constructionist/postmodern views. In response to several scholars' call for more holistic and better integrated approaches to theorizing and researching identity (Bernstein 2005; Erickson 1995; Frable 1997; Howard 2000), this study is predicated on a conception of self that is both multidimensional and unified, both changing and somewhat stable. Although the identities of the couple partners are often fluid and situational, they also take into account the continuing significance of cultural groups and nations that, although certainly not homogeneous or unitary, are often perceived or imagined as such. These assumed cultural entities become signifiers of "otherness," constructed as having come from another or different "social or biological stock" (Yuval-Davis 1997, 47). This chapter thus takes up the question raised by Mary Bernstein (2005):

"Why, given the insights of social constructionism and postmodernism, are identities invoked and/or felt as if they were essentialist?" (60).

In their interviews and narratives, most of the couple partners recognized transformations of cultural self-identity that they attributed to living with a person from a different culture, but embedded in that recognition was the essentializing of the other partner's culture that often involved stereotyping or attributing certain characteristics to the partner's entire cultural group. As the following sections will demonstrate, while intercultural partnerships allow persons to cross cultures and to incorporate aspects of the other's cultural identity, the partners also construct these shifting identities against at least somewhat stable and monolithic perceptions of the "other."

Recognizing Cultural Differences

All of the couples included in this study were conscious of dissimilarities separating the partners that were more than just differences of personality. Identified most often as cultural differences, the dissimilarities were perceived as significant sometimes in the early and sometimes in the later stages of the relationships.

Attraction to Difference

In some cases, perceived cultural differences were what initially attracted the partners to each other. Such initial differences appeared salient especially to the international couples, who comprised 55 percent of the sample (or twenty-one of the thirty-eight couples).

Belinda (U.S.-born of European heritage) and Luiz (a native of El Salvador) were mutually attracted because they saw each other as distinct from potential mates in their respective cultures. The couple met when Belinda and a group of relief workers came to Luiz's village to build a health center.

> LUIZ: I saw that she was trying to do something in a country that she doesn't even belong to or anything, and I thought that was very interesting.... I saw girls from my own country, and it was different.... I didn't find them interesting.

BELINDA: I feel like a lot of men here [in the United States], I would never have been able to marry or have a relationship with.... I was attracted to [Luiz] because he was fighting to improve the world; he and I share[d] a sense of what community should be like.... I felt much more in tune with that than I did here.

Similarly, Jerry (Anglo-American from the Midwest) was attracted to Hege (Norwegian) in part because he found her to be very different from the American women he had known.

JERRY: I was very happy to meet her and I loved the simple, frank, honest way that Norwegians approach people and life. This to me was refreshing and new.... We went out [to the house he was renting] one weekend and she thought the kitchen needed tidying up, so she was down on her hands and knees mopping the floor. I thought, "I don't know any American girl who would do that!" There is a difference.

Hege, who had traveled extensively by the time she met Jerry, was drawn to him because he was considerably older and from another country.

HEGE: I had kind of overdosed on dating boys my own age. I was looking for some kind of drama. [Jerry] was older and interesting. Because he was American, from another part of the world, added to the drama.

Casey (U.S.-born of Anglo European heritage) was attracted to Eva (Honduran) because he expected her to be different from women he knew in the United States.

CASEY: I think I just got kind of bored with American girls.... American women would be less likely to be [in a] viable lifetime relationship.... I expected to have a better chance to be in a long, stable relationship [with a woman from a Latin American country]

Eva, on the other hand, was happy to meet an American whom she found to be "less macho" than the men in her home culture.

Debbie (Anglo-American Christian), who married Walid (Lebanese Muslim), found her partner interesting because of the qualities she perceived in Middle Eastern men.

> DEBBIE: They [Middle Eastern men] tend to be much more straightforward and fearless and honest than American men. I value that directness and self-confidence.

Similarly, Susan (Jewish American of eastern European heritage) was attracted to Samorn (a native of Burma and a Buddhist) because of characteristics she attributed to men from Asian cultures.

> SUSAN: I find Asian men in general to be very gentle.... There's the non-aggressiveness of these people, the spirituality of the people; and he had all of those [qualities], and that was very attractive to me.

A study of American women who married Japanese men similarly found that the women were attracted to Japanese men's perceived "quality of being serious, dependable and steady," while often simultaneously recognizing the lack of such virtues in American men (Diggs 2001, 11).

In some cases, a perception (usually by white partners) of the other as "exotic" fueled the initial attraction. In the preceding chapter, we saw how Russell perceived Suzy's physical appearance as exotic and appealing. Likewise, Stephanie (U.S. Midwest-born of Scandinavian heritage) found Claudia's (indigenous Brazilian) nationality and physical appearance very attractive.

> STEPHANIE: When my friend introduced us she said that [Claudia] was from Brazil and I immediately had this very positive, warm feeling about her. And she looked kind of exotic ... the swept up dark hair, brown skin, and high cheekbones.

European American Jessica was drawn to her Chinese American partner, Tony, because,

When I first met him, he didn't say much. He didn't try to impress me. He just looked at me with such a deep, mysterious, exotic look. I found that really different and appealing.

Maria Root also reports that perceived exoticism was sometimes part of the initial attraction between the interracial couples she interviewed (Root 2001). And in her edited volume, *Cross-Border Marriages: Gender and Mobility in Transnational Asia* (2005), Nicole Constable suggests that marriages between Asians and westerners "both reflect and are propelled by fantasies and imaginings about gender, sexuality, tradition and modernity" (7).

Difference as Initial Deterrent

For some couples, initial perceptions of difference, particularly race, impeded an attachment. George (Tanzanian) and Nancy (U.S.-born, Italian American) waited close to a year before they decided to be more than just friends.

GEORGE: We were both very cautious, we took things slow.... We knew from the start that we were from such different places, that we had very different upbringings and experiences, so I think that was what kept us from jumping into a more intimate relationship. And, of course, there was the race issue.

NANCY: There was a period between when we were first interested in each other and the second time we went out, ... when we saw each other at sort of mutual things where we were just kind of friends and maybe flirting a little bit. There was no serious contact between the initial encounter and then it was about four or five months later [when they went out on a date]. A lot of that had to do with my reticence about the fact that he was not only from a different culture but [also] from a different race.

Mae (African American from Southern U.S.) and Penny (Irish-American from the Northeast) also waited a while before allowing their friendship to turn into an intimate relationship.

MAE: I noticed that she is of a different race, and I must admit that was a bit of a problem for me because I'd never been with a white woman before. But I liked her right away. There was something interesting about her.... It definitely was an attraction, though I didn't realize it until later. At first, I thought I just liked her a lot, and we became fast friends. It took about five or six months before I knew that it was something more, more than just a close friendship.

PENNY: I liked [Mae] instantly. We were friends almost from the minute we started talking. We just hit it off like that. I remember thinking about a month after I met her, "Could this be more than friendship?" But I sort of shrugged it off, in part because she was from the South and we came from such different backgrounds. And, let's face it, I couldn't imagine then being intimate with a black woman.

Japanese American Suzy, who married Polish American Russell after a long courtship, initially kept him at bay despite a strong attraction between them.

SUZY: I had never dated a non-Asian man before, and he [had] never dated an Asian woman, so we took it very slow. That was very hard because I had strong feelings for him from the beginning, but I was afraid of getting involved with someone who wouldn't understand my culture. My sister had a relationship with an Italian American, and that didn't work out, and I was thinking that it wouldn't work out for us either.

Russell also was hesitant.

When we first met she told me that even though she was born here [in the United States] she grew up very Japanese and never dated anyone who was not from her culture. I was like, "Should I even pursue this?" But I was really attracted to her, and liked her, and wanted to see her, so we saw each other just as friends for a while, a long while actually.

Recognition of Differences in Later Stages of Relationships

In some cases, cultural differences were not perceived to be significant at first but emerged later, once the couple had been living together for some time. Leslie (U.S.-born midwesterner of British heritage who converted from Christianity to Judaism) and David (U.S.-born Jew who lived on an Israeli kibbutz for many years), resided in a spiritual commune in the early stage of their marriage. Only later, when Leslie became pregnant with their first child, did they begin to recognize cultural differences.

> LESLIE: Early on we didn't see many cultural differences because we were living in the [commune] and were both sort of committed to communal living and had . . . similar ways of thinking about relationships and the world in general. When we decided to live by ourselves, as a family, when we started having children, . . . here's where the cultural thing comes in. . . . He had this ideal view of the [kibbutz] where he grew up and so he really wanted to be part of a collective. He believes that collective living is [a] much more economical and rational way to live. I agree in theory, but in practice it was hard for me to continue to live like that after we were married and especially once we decided to have children. . . . For him, the whole community, the collective would be like a family, but for me, my husband and kids are family . . . a family needs its own space. I guess it's the way I was brought up and what I know.

> DAVID: For a while [Leslie] was open to having other people living with us. . . . I felt that if we were going to raise kids, we had to have many adult models around, kind of like in the kibbutz. [Their first child] grew up with having other people living in our apartment, which I thought was great. [Leslie] had a hard time with it. She was happy to move. I really wasn't happy. I still have that [unhappiness].

Andrew (American of East European heritage) and Mady (born and raised in the Netherlands) met and lived together for the first two years of their relationship in a college environment. They began to notice cultural differences later when they married and had a child.

> ANDREW: At first I wasn't really too concerned about those kinds of things [cultural differences]. We began to see [cultural] differences once we became more established, once we started a family, and when we started to deal with parents, and brothers and sisters.

Andrew explains that he and his spouse discovered over time that they related very differently to their families—for her, family members could do no wrong and she was never critical of them, while he was more direct and confrontational. The partners also had different notions about how to raise their son; Mady was very permissive and Andrew took on a disciplinarian role. Andrew saw these dissimilarities as cultural because, he reasoned, they came from upbringing and experiences in distinct cultural groups. Mady, who initially thought that any differences between them were probably due to "personality clashes," upon further reflection stated:

Eventually I could see that there's some cultural difference to how we approach life. I've definitely been brought up in a community that valued close families and I still have that [value]. . . . In Holland most people I knew were very open to children and punishment was not used.

Similarly, Michael (Jewish American of British heritage) and Joe (Cuban American), although aware they were from very different cultures, did not pay attention to differences until they had lived together for a while.

> MICHAEL: At first we didn't notice the differences, but once we started to settle into the relationship things became more apparent. [Joe] has a cultural temperament that is very different from mine. I'm much more reserved and self-sufficient. He needs other people, social stimulation, more than I do. I can spend days by myself, or only with him, and be totally happy.

JOE: After a few months of living together, I started to see some differences of a cultural nature. In Cuban culture there's a lot of socializing and I was used to going out all the time and having people over, just spending a lot of time with friends. [Michael] prefers to spend time just with me or even by himself. He really values his privacy and doesn't like people intruding. That's how he was raised. His family is very British.

Cultural Differences Activated by Return to Culture of Origin

Sometimes, a bicultural or multicultural spouse's "(an)other" culture was activated when the couple returned temporarily to that spouse's cultural environment. Elizabeth (Czech American, Catholic, who spent several years studying in France) did not regard her husband Raj (Algerian-born Muslim) as very different culturally until they visited his Arabic family and community in Algiers.

ELIZABETH: I don't think I even realized how much of a difference there was [between us] until I actually went to the country. I kept viewing [Raj] as European because I had no exposure to an African country. He had European interests—French music, food; we speak English and French together—he didn't have Arabic friends much of the time [in the United States], so I didn't see him as being very much different from Europeans until I went to [Algeria]. He has a <u>double culture</u>, and [in the United States] I would naturally be more exposed to the side of him that was more Westernized.

When asked how differently her husband acted when they were in Algeria, Elizabeth recounts that he was very deferential to elders (including his older brother), communicated more subtly through body language than he did in the United States, and requested that she always go places with him, cover her legs, and spend time with the women, as most activities were gender-segregated. Raj, who had lived first in France and then in the United States for over ten years, acknowledges that he is well aware of how different his culture is in

Algeria and sees himself "slipping back into it" whenever he returns with his wife.

Anna (born and raised in Russia) and Robert (U.S.-born Anglo-American) also find that when they visit Anna's family in Russia, their cultural differences become more salient to them.

> ROBERT: I think I became more conscious of this the first time we went back to [Russia], . . . I could see her operate on her own turf. . . . [Before that] I could never say that I know who this person is totally because I didn't know where she was coming from, how she would be around her friends, her family, where she can really spew out what she's saying, where she understands the jokes. . . . Even though I didn't know what's going on, I could see her, what's going on in her. It was clearly her world, a very different world from mine.

Anna, who also tried initially to deny that there were significant cultural differences between her and her spouse ("We had common interests in literature and art, and I could talk to him about intellectual things; I didn't see many differences at first"), recognizes them more whenever she returns to Russia.

> ANNA: When I go back and then . . . [return here] I really see how differently we live and, to some extent, how differently I act. . . . I'm more relaxed when I'm in [Russia]. I also see that I, and other [Russians], relate differently to family and friends. This bothers me, when I return . . . and notice more that [Robert] and many of our friends are so disconnected from their parents, their families.

Anita (Puerto Rican-born American) and Burt (white, U.S.-born midwesterner of European heritage) also discovered cultural differences after they settled into their marriage.

> BURT: Most of our cultural differences came out some time after we were married. We did not recognize [them] because we

met in a common context, sort of neutral territory, not really where she grew up, not really where I grew up, and our relationship came out of that. Then, after you're married... much more comes out about your values and the way you see things and all of that. For example, the views of family—we had extremely different views.... In Puerto Rican culture, family is the extended kin. And where I grew up, I had no concept of that.... Family was strictly nuclear family... and the idea of extended family was beyond me.

Burt recalls how he was "confronted with the fact that [Anita] was from a totally different culture, in a very dramatic sense." The "confrontation" took place in two stages.

BURT: We went to this baptism of a cousin, at a cousin's house, over in [an east coast city], and the entire day there was nobody else around who was Anglo but me. And I call this my immersion experience because the entire day I was totally immersed in a different language, different traditions, everything was different.... Another time [he experienced cultural difference directly] was our first trip to Puerto Rico as a married couple.... We arrived, and we got in a little car,... and we drove like eight hours up into the mountains,... and we got to this little town and it seemed like thousands of people were in the plaza. And there's a narrow street, houses are backed up—little bitty shacks are backed up to each other on both sides of the road, and then we come to a halt. And suddenly the overwhelming feeling set in... this is a home? And the house is like eight feet wide... and everybody's outside and there's no Anglo in sight, and no one even speaks English, except for the people I'm with.... And then it's like, this is entirely different! So those two experiences stand out to me as a kind of two-by-four to the head, saying this: "Wow, she really comes from a different culture."

For Anita, it also was culture shock when she first visited Burt's parents in their mid-American, rural town.

ANITA: His family was detached and stiff midwesterners. We always kid about his family reunions. You line up thirty people in a room and nobody's talking, everybody's absolutely quiet. You know, "How's the corn?" There's no yelling. Very different than what I was used to. With my family, everybody's speaking at once, and everything's loud, and there's music, and food, and everything all at once.

Commonalities Trump Differences

Sometimes couples expected differences between the partners because they came from what they thought to be very different cultures, yet found, despite their differences, that they had more in common culturally than they had assumed. For instance, Sarah (U.S.-born, Jewish, European American) and Frank (U.S.-born Egyptian Arab, Christian) although of different backgrounds and religions, found much cultural common ground.

SARAH: What really struck me, the more I learned about my husband's family's history and their values, is how very similar his family, his community, was to mine.... For example, both [Frank] and I come from places where people are in the habit of constantly observing and scrutinizing others, where it's not possible to do something without somebody commenting on it.... It's a type of meddling, an interference of sorts that is very emotionally charged. It was in both our communities.

FRANK: We come from homes where lots of time is spent around the kitchen table talking about people, all the family and friends, examining intimate relationships and events in great detail. People tell stories of the past and embellish them, so each time a story's retold it becomes richer and more complicated. We both grew up with that.

Selma (Mexican American) and Banu (Asian-Indian American), a same-sex couple we learned about in the previous chapter, also were surprised to discover similarities in their families and communities of origin.

BANU: I was amazed that her mother had very similar attitudes to my mother, especially about motherhood and just a woman's role in the family—very traditional. And that seems to be the way that her mother's friends are, too, from the area where she grew up. At first I thought she would feel very uncomfortable around my traditional family, but later I realized that that's what she experienced also.

SELMA: It turned out that we both came from pretty traditional types of families and neighborhoods with fathers heads of households and mothers who did everything in the house regardless if they worked or not, where people had much the same ideas about how to raise children, and so on. The specific customs and such differed a lot, but there was that basic similarity.

Although Banu and Selma have left their communities of origin and are far from traditional in how they live as a couple, the similar aspects of their backgrounds provide a shared understanding in how they relate to their families.

The couples in this study perceive cultural differences between the partners in different degrees and as more or less salient sometimes early and sometimes later in their relationships. In all cases, the acknowledgement of difference entails the perception that there are somewhat stable, recognizable aspects of cultures residing within individuals and that one's culture of origin, at least partially if not dramatically, diverges from that of one's partner. As a number of the above excerpts from interviews attest, the respondents often resort to stereotypes when describing cultural differences, making generalizations about people of a particular ethnic or national background. It is also important to note that most of the cultural differences the study participants recognize focus on relations with family members; this aspect of intercultural couples' lives is of great importance to them, as family reactions can cause considerable strain or lend understanding and support (Childs 2005; Durodoye and Coker 2008; Root 2001; Spickard 1989).

Under what circumstances do cultural differences become significant for intercultural couples and how do they affect the partners' individual identities and their relational identity as a couple? How does the couples' social environment mediate the process of identity reinvention? I address these questions in the following sections.

When Cultural Differences Matter

The importance of the differences perceived by intercultural partners varies among the couples and changes from one time to another for specific couples. Whether partners see differences between them as highly important or insignificant seems to depend on the specific circumstances of the couple. In a diverse, multicultural setting where both partners have access to others from their respective cultural groups, differences matter less than when the couple lives in an environment where one or both partners feel marginalized. Moreover, support from or rejection by the partners' families of origin is frequently a factor in the process.

Carlie (African-American Christian) and Gary (Jewish American of East European heritage), one of the couples whose narratives I included in this study, have been married twenty-one years. The partners lived for a time in a cosmopolitan community on the East Coast and found in that environment that their marriage was readily accepted and posed no impediments.

> GARY: Few seemed to take much notice of our relationship, and when someone did it was usually positive. We both had multiracial circles of friends that included mixed-race and multicultural couples. And we both had involvements in progressive social and political activities, where racial and cultural understanding were sought after and respected.... The people we [knew] and respect[ed], shared with and depended on, were all supportive (Tartakov and Tartakov 1994, 147–48).

When the couple moved to a small midwestern town, however, they became more conscious of differences once they discovered they were an anomaly.

CARLIE: We moved from a community that was relatively open and tolerant of mixed marriages to one we perceive as not.... [In the midwestern town] we were now often the only mixed couple at most of the work-related and social events we went to.... We feel that people who are unaccepting of our relationship are suspicious of our motives. A certain amount of disrespect is shown.... Our differences was not an issue for us until we were [confronted by] the wider community (151–52).

For this couple, the constant support of both partners' families of origin, albeit at a distance, and a circle of close friends, helped them withstand an unwelcoming environment. With a shift in social context from majority to minority group status, social affirmation becomes especially important as a way to counteract the negative effects of the stigmatizing environment (Ichiyama et al. 1996; Orbe and Harris 2001).

Anita (Puerto Rican-born American) and Burt (European American from the Midwest) lived for most of the twenty-five years of their married life in predominantly white, middle-class communities as Burt, a minister, kept getting assigned to white churches.

BURT: Because Christian churches in America are so segregated by race, there were not statistically significant presences of minorities in any of the churches I was assigned.... Most of our marriage has been in that [all-white] setting, and [Anita] has had to deal with being the "other one."

ANITA: They always saw me as different.... [A]t the same time they demanded that... those of us who aren't from the mainstream culture... relinquish some of who we are.... And [Burt] and I have very different views... our ways of viewing the world and being in the world are very different.

Since this couple moved around a great deal, even though Anita felt close to her family of origin, her family could not provide enough support from afar to offset Anita's sense of marginalization. However, the couple began to both de-emphasize and accept their differences when they moved to a multicultural, multiracial neighborhood in a large city.

> ANITA: Living here is finally comfortable for me. I can be more myself, am not expected to fit in with the others, to give up parts of myself.

> BURT: We now live in a culturally diverse world.... When I look around at our friends and people we get together with, where we live, ... we no longer stand out, and our differences don't seem as important.

Lee (Chinese American) and Roy (of mixed African American and American Indian heritage), same-sex partners who have lived together for seven years, despite coming from very different cultural backgrounds, are able to stay together without much attention to their differences because of the great diversity of their community and closest friends.

> ROY: We wouldn't survive this long if we lived in the kinds of places where each of us grew up [racially segregated ethnic neighborhoods of large U.S. cities]. Being part of a community where you have every kind of person represented—African Americans, Chicanos, Asians, Indians, Whites, gay, straight, transgender, you name it—there's just this tolerance of differences and real acceptance of people for who they are.... Even though [Lee] and I come from very different cultures, it doesn't seem to matter when everybody you see most of the time is also different. Difference is kind of normal where we live; it's taken for granted.

> LEE: As a gay man living with someone from a totally different background and different race, when I think about it, I'm amazed sometimes that we don't notice the differences more. But then almost everybody that we know, all our closest friends, our neighbors, people who live in our neighborhood, they're all different from the American mainstream—White, Anglo, heterosexual, middle-class mainstream. I guess we do have some straight Whites, but they're not in the majority here.

For this couple, whose families of origin have rejected them because of their sexual orientation, an accepting social environment is crucial to their positive sense of being together.

Belinda (European American who grew up on the East Coast) and Luiz (Salvadoran), after living the first two years of their relationship in El Salvador, moved to a southern U.S. state where both felt disconnected from their previous cultural roots.

> LUIZ: I can't really be myself here. There [in his village in El Salvador] everybody knows me, I know everybody, I know the culture, I know what to say and what not to say. And here sometimes I feel like I have a block, I have rules to follow, but I'm not sure why I shouldn't do or say something.
>
> BELINDA: The South is such a different culture from where I'm from [in the East], and I just don't feel connected here. . . . I didn't want to stay here. . . . Neither of us felt like we were really living here. So we kind of lived in this limbo for about two years.

Lacking support for their own cultures or acceptance as an intercultural couple, and being separated from their families of origin and friends, both partners felt marginalized and became more conscious of their differences.

> BELINDA: I wanted to go back to [the east coast city where she once lived] because that's where all my friends are. And I'm a lot closer with many of my friends than I am with immediate family members, which he couldn't understand. Because . . . there in his village . . . it's all family.
>
> LUIZ: It is a different culture [here] I live the American style. I just got my little family here, my wife, and my kids, . . . and I don't even practice any of the things that I used to do.

However, this couple, like Anita and Burt, began to be less concerned about cultural differences between the partners once they moved to a multicultural, working-class neighborhood where many of their neighbors were Latinos/as and Whites from outside the South.

Japanese American Suzy and Polish American Russell left their respective ethnic communities when they married and moved to a large city in the Midwest. As we have seen, living in a predominantly white, newly constructed suburb and lacking support for their cultures, the couple felt alienated and turned attention to the differences between them.

> SUZY: The first three years when we lived in [the suburb], we constantly had misunderstandings and disagreements because we thought we were so different. And because there weren't other Japanese around, I couldn't show [Russell] that the things I did and how I thought was not just weird, but that it was part of who I was because of how I was raised in my culture.

> RUSSELL: I really missed all the [Polish] stuff I was used to—the food, the socializing late into the night, the loudness and vibrancy of the culture. And I couldn't do that with [Suzy] because she wasn't really into that kind of food, and didn't like loud parties, and there weren't other people around who were from the same background as me.

The pair eventually met and befriended people from both of their ethnic groups and moved to an area of town that was more diverse.

> RUSSELL: Now we have some Japanese and Polish friends and also some from other cultures and that really helps me, helps us, be more ourselves and not to be so defensive about our cultures.... We know that our cultures are different but it's OK that we're different—it's not a big deal any more.

> SUZY: I think we pay less attention to the differences now. The neighborhood where we live, there are so many mixed couples, and nobody singles us out.... We have close friends who come from our cultures and our families come to visit more often and we visit them, too.

Hence, for this couple as for many others, a supportive community, friends, and family serve to diminish the importance of the problematic or divisive aspects of cultural differences.

Significance of Perceived Cultural Differences for Cultural Identity

As indicated above, the social context within which a couple finds itself has consequences for how the partners perceive their differences. In supportive environments, couples value their differences but do not see them as highly important to their lives together. On the other hand, in contexts where one or both partners feel unaccepted or marginal, dissimilarities are often exacerbated and create tensions between them.

How differences are perceived has consequences for the partners' individual identities and their identity as a couple. Thus, couples such as Anita and Burt, who were constantly reminded of their differences throughout most of their married life together, have very distinct identities based on the perception of being culturally different from each other.

ANITA: I fought to be recognized for who I was without having to give up something.... I'm a warm, loving, caring person.... The way I express myself, my loudness, my expressiveness is cultural.... He [is] much more detached, stiff midwesterner.

BURT: In the culture I grew up in, you don't express affect.... I've grown up with a model that adulthood was being totally independent and separate from others. That's been an important aspect of who I am.

Anita and Burt also strongly identify as an intercultural couple and in their separate interviews emphasize their cultural differences as a source of conflict between them.

Belinda and Luiz, as seen above, also started to identify more with their respective cultures when they lived in a predominantly white, Southern community and viewed cultural differences as causing problems in their marriage. Similarly, Russell and Suzy indicate that they were more keenly aware of their cultural identities when they lived in an isolated, white suburban neighborhood that lacked support for their respective cultures and for them as an intercultural couple.

On the other hand, couples that live in ethnically and racially diverse areas recognize cultural differences, but view them as less important to their individual identities and their identity as a couple and tend to emphasize commonalities between the partners. Lee and Roy, the pair who reside in a highly diverse metropolitan neighborhood, state that they seldom notice that one partner is Chinese American and the other African American/American Indian and see instead other factors as more salient to their identities.

> ROY: At the same time that I'm, of course, aware of being non-white and living in a racist society, and that I'm from a very different culture than [Lee], these things are less important to me as a person, as an individual, than that I've made something of my life, that I achieved something.... And we together, we don't really identify as an interracial couple, so much, I mean, we are aware of it, but we don't pay much attention to it on a daily basis.... I think we identify more with what we have in common, like our interests in art [they collect local art and antiques] and our political interests.

> LEE: My cultural heritage will always be with me, but it's not so crucial any more to how I see myself. I see myself primarily as a person who can live among people of different races and cultures and be comfortable with that.... As a couple, I think [Roy] and I also don't dwell on the different cultural aspects; we focus more on things that unite us, our hobbies and our commitments to social issues.

Similarly, Jessica (European American) and Tony (Chinese American), who have resided the entire seventeen years of their married life in a very diverse, multicultural college town, emphasize what they have in common and do not perceive their differences as highly important to their identities.

TONY: I don't really think much about our cultural differences, that I'm from a Chinese background and she's from [a] European [background].... The differences are there, but sort of in the background.... Most of the time I notice more the ways we are alike, what we share; like we enjoy cooking together and working on the garden.

JESSICA: [Tony] comes from a very different cultural background..., but I don't notice it much anymore. Only when his parents come to visit, then he starts acting more Chinese—he gets more formal, more deferential.... We have a lot in common, interests and activities that we do together.

Carlie (African-American Christian) and Gary (Jewish American of East European heritage), having lived in both supportive and less accepting environments, strive to develop a balance between recognizing their differences and finding similarities that foster their identity as a couple. Carlie, who joined a historically black church, got involved in singing Gospel music, and has been active in the NAACP, points out that Gary has his own groups and activities as well while they also attend together some of each other's events. Additionally, the couple has social causes and organizations in which both partners are involved and they "share friends and activities" (Tartakov and Tartakov 1994, 151). And Gary confirms,

> As with many things, we've found that the key has been acceptance and respect of each other's interests [and backgrounds], not conversion ... [but we also share] a very direct interest in the social world around us. We are both activists. (152–54).

This pair does not see their different cultural identities as sources of conflict but rather as contributing to the enrichment of each partner and to both as a couple.

Among couples in which one partner is from the dominant U.S. racial and ethnic group (White, Christian, European American) and the other from a foreign country (especially non-Western), a historically underrepresented group in the United States (African American, Asian, Latino/a), and/or from a minority religious group (Jewish, Muslim),[1] cultural differences typically are perceived as more important by the minority group partner, regardless of the social circumstances of the couple. This is especially so when the dominant group partner is male.[2] Cultural identity also is more clearly expressed by the partners with minority status. Contrary to some predictions that the minority partner will assimilate to the culture of the majority counterpart (Alba 1986; Barron 1972; Gordon 1964), minority partners in this study resist assimilation. Holding onto (essentialist) identities is related to the political context in which particular identity categories have been "repressed, delegitimized or devalued in dominant discourse" (Calhoun 1995, 18), circumstances where minority group members tend to use their cultural identities to challenge negative representations (Bernstein 2005).

Paul (U.S.-born of European heritage) and Emma (Pakistani), despite both having lived for periods of time in other countries besides the United States and Pakistan, differ markedly in how they perceive their cultural differences. Emma has no trouble identifying several cultural dissimilarities between herself and her spouse, including orientations toward family, attitudes toward privacy and work, and gender expectations. Paul, on the other hand, although acknowledging that he and Emma are definitely from different cultures, after much prodding is able to point to one concrete difference: "how [Emma] holds the fork," which he saw as cultural because "I've noticed it with other members of her culture as well." Although Emma recognizes that with time she is starting to accommodate to her partner's culture ("The longer I live here, the longer I'm married to an American, I'm aware of the compromises . . . I'm immersed in the mainstream U.S. culture twenty-four hours of the day"), she actively resists assimilation.

EMMA: I am now beginning to notice in myself a respect for the traditional—traditional [Pakistani] anything, including the language—and I don't know if I feel threatened by my marriage to an American. . . . Is it part of my identity that's threatened? I've certainly not taken on [Paul's last name] after marriage. . . . It could just be that having made the decision that this is going

Reinventing Cultural Identity

to be my home, that then I want to salvage what I can of what I have let go of. And that is why I think I suddenly want to celebrate the holidays more, like the Muslim holiday of the Eid. I've become very resistant to Christmas and Easter, and . . . part of it is that I've never celebrated any religious holidays and so why would I now want to be roped into Christmas?

Similarly, Anna (Russian) recognizes significant cultural differences between herself and her spouse. Robert (Anglo-American) admits that at first he tended to ignore their cultural differences as he focused on commonalities, and only several years into the marriage began to entertain that "there was some cultural stuff here." Meanwhile, as Anna begins to function better in her adopted culture, she steadfastly holds onto her Russian identity.

ANNA: I'll always be [Russian]. . . . In nine or ten years I will reach the age where I'll be half of my life in the U.S. and half in [Russia], so I can say I'm as much [Russian] as American. But the roots of a child, the genes are [Russian]. If I took out American citizenship it wouldn't change anything. Calling myself American is not a goal.

Anna also maintains her cultural identity by retaining her foreign-sounding accent: "I have an accent, and I guess I kind of like having something a little different."

Burt and Anita demonstrate a similar pattern. Although both recognize cultural differences between them, it is clear that Anita places more emphasis on these differences because she is the one expected to "relinquish aspects of who [I am]."

ANITA: I think that [Burt] has always assumed I am much more—that I, in fact, am from mainstream U.S. culture. And therefore, there's a little intolerance on his part. . . . My reality of having lived in a racist society and having to deal with some things has given me a different edge than I think [Burt] really knows—or that he really acknowledges affected me. . . . I don't think he is aware of the battles I've fought to be my own person.

[72]

To remain "herself," Anita keeps her Hispanic last name, maintains her knowledge of Spanish, does not join any of Burt's Protestant churches, and "draw[s] very strict limits about what people can expect, and not [expect], of me."

Shana (Jewish American of East European heritage), married to Dirk (Christian German-American), is highly aware of cultural differences in her marriage (childrearing approaches, importance of orderliness, attitudes toward the Holocaust), while her spouse does not perceive most of the couple's differences to be cultural. In her interview, Shana talks at length about the aspects of her culture that she consciously preserves while living with Dirk.

> SHANA: There are the holidays. Definitely Seder, Passover, which as a child I perceived to be the most important holiday. . . . I still do Hanukah, I fast Yom Kippur, Rosh Hashanah. I don't go to temple very often. . . . If I do go to a service it feels good, it feels nice. It's like those little pulls on your ties. . . . I just find that the older I get, . . . I'm really so pleased that I'm a Jew; . . . there's an ethical fiber, just a sense toward humanity that's very Jewish. I identify with [that] more and more.

Isabela (Chilean) also recognizes many cultural differences (food preferences, relations with family members, customs and holidays, childrearing practices) between herself and her Irish American husband of fifteen years, Graham, while he notes only one area of difference (childrearing). She resists assimilating into her spouses' mainstream culture by taking advantage of the availability of foods and magazines from her country and modern technologies that help to bridge the physical distance.

> ISABELA: I make an effort to buy avocados and other ingredients for [Chilean] dishes. And I keep in touch through magazines. I watch the news from [Chile] just about every day. And luckily . . . we [now] have a lot more access. . . . Next week we're gonna have the video conference—maybe I'll be able to see people on the screen from now on... letters are kind of obsolete now. . . . My culture, that's like the major thing to me. It's that sore spot in my heart . . . that's always there.

Ron (African American) and Greg (American of Irish heritage), who have lived together for more than ten years, mostly in a racially and culturally mixed neighborhood, do not perceive significant cultural differences between them (though Ron spoke of more cultural issues in his interview). Although Greg has no definite sense of cultural identity ("By the time I met Ron, my cultural heritage was not that important to me"), Ron clearly identifies as African American.

> RON: Because I haven't been part of a separate African American community for so long, I've lost that sense of tradition or something. But I still see myself as an African American man. I share with other African Americans our troubled history in this country, the racism, the prejudice we've had to endure. For me it's a cultural and a political identity.

The above examples illustrate how white male privilege operates even in intercultural relationships where the dominant group partner is usually accepting of and sensitive to the culture of the minority group partner. Being in a privileged position, the white, European American male partners are more likely to overlook cultural differences and to take their own cultural identity for granted.[3] The minority group partners, in contradistinction, are much more aware of their cultural backgrounds and how these differ from those of their mates and, consequently, they more consciously express their cultural identities.

Not all dominant group partners are equally dismissive of the cultural differences that their minority group partners identified. Those who are more in agreement with their partners are also more likely to be exposed to or immersed in the culture of their mates. Thus, for example, Burt (Anita's spouse), who recognizes many of the same differences that she articulates, had spent time with her U.S. relatives and made several visits with her to Puerto Rico. Similarly, Robert (Anna's spouse) lived for a time in Russia and periodically visits Anna's family with her.

Relational Identities

Over time, most of the couples who participated in this study became less concerned with cultural differences between the partners and their identities assumed an increasingly "hybrid" character that both underscored and blurred cultural boundaries (Bhaba 1994). This simultaneous recognition and merging of cultural differences can be viewed as the construction of relational identities. Although such hybrid identity formation is most apparent in couples where both partners are from nondominant groups or when the dominant group partner is female, even in dominant male/minority group couples the crossing and merging of cultures is evident.

We have already seen in the previous chapter that Selma's (Mexican American) and Banu's (Asian-Indian American) partnership exemplifies how cultural identities can be both retained and hybridized. Selma makes clear that "She's very respectful of my culture, and I am of hers. We're both interested in learning more about each other's cultures." Banu, for her part, readily admits that "I've learned so much about Mexican Americans, their culture . . . from living with [Selma] and being around her family, that I feel that her culture is starting to be part of my being, alongside my Indian part, and the more Americanized part." Suzy (Japanese American) and Russell (Polish American) also found that over time they both retained and have started to merge aspects of each other's cultures.

> SUZY: I now know so much more about [Russell's] culture and he about mine, and so we can now kind of go back and forth between them . . . without much of a problem. It feels very natural for us to visit [each other's] families and to participate in different customs, holidays, and all that without having to give up anything. Because I'm still feeling Japanese and he has that Polish background, but we also are a little of the other culture, some of the other culture is also now part of each of us.
>
> RUSSELL: I guess that because of my marriage I am able to have a real appreciation of another culture and to feel like I'm also part of that culture in some way. And I'm still connected to my Pol-

Reinventing Cultural Identity

ish heritage.... I now have two cultures, well, actually three, because I'm also, of course, an American and partake of the general American culture, too.

Salvadoran Luiz and European American Belinda also eventually began to view themselves as cultural hybrids and to appreciate the advantages of being able to function in more than one culture.

LUIZ: I feel now that I can live here [United States] and I can live there [El Salvador], too. I know enough of each culture to get along.... I've come to know both ways.

BELINDA: Even before Luiz and I were married, I knew his culture well since I lived two years in [El Salvador]. I felt very comfortable there. But life is easier in some ways here, so I see the positives here and there, and the negatives.... I can move from one culture to the other pretty easily.

Leila (Jewish American of eastern European heritage) and James (Mexican American, nonpracticing Catholic), while living in a predominantly Jewish community, have incorporated some of each other's cultures into their individual identities.

JAMES: Although I haven't converted, because most of our friends now are Jewish, we live in a mostly Jewish neighborhood, and are all involved in the temple, I sort of feel like an honorary Jew.... A part of me is still Mexican. For one thing, I can't change my skin color, and I wouldn't want to. And also, I don't forget where I come from and the positive things I got from my culture. But... the Jewish culture has become much more integral to me.

LEILA: I'm perceived differently. I believe I'm an enigma to some people ... they are eager to figure out just what I am. I purposefully hyphenate my last name [the first part is Jewish and the second part Hispanic], and so people have a hard time classifying me. I don't like neat compartments, I defy them.... I think this has liberated me from a lot of my own tendency to get sucked into some cultural category. So although I identify primarily as a Jew, I'm sort of a multicultural one.

Carlie (African-American Christian) and Gary (Jewish American of East European background), although retaining their cultural identities, also have deepened their appreciation and acceptance of each other's cultures.

CARLIE: We have retained our individual [cultural] identities. Neither [of us] expects or desires that the other live solely in one culture or the other . . . we've been able to move in many different communities. . . . We find ourselves shifting back and forth among different groups [African American, Jewish, East European, and dominant White European-American]. We feel enriched by the different communities we've shared (Tartakov and Tartakov 1994, 151).

GARY: We have not tried to homogenize our backgrounds or bury them. . . . If anything, our personal cultural interests have grown somewhat out of interest in not losing touch with our own histories [and heritages]. . . . I'd say we've been both respectful and celebrators of the differences (152).

Puerto Rican-born Anita and European American Burt, after many years of struggling with their differences, developed separate identities by drawing on aspects of their own and each other's cultures.

ANITA: I can take some of the pieces that I think make for my understanding about the world that . . . come from my background and others from my experiences in the mainstream world. . . . I feel like I'm able to live in two culturally different worlds.

BURT: We live in a . . . culturally diverse world and have that kind of view that other couples who didn't cross the boundaries [do not have]. I've become aware how my self-identity has been affected by all this [being married to someone from a different culture]. After I was appointed here [to a church in a multicultural neighborhood], a black woman [a member of the church] said to me: "I'm glad we didn't get somebody who was all white." And clearly, supposedly, I'm all white, . . . but [because of who his wife is], I'm not *all* white.

And Greg (Irish American), who has lived with Ron (African American) for twelve years, has this to say about how his identity has been affected by their relationship:

> GREG: I've become more appreciative of African American culture and Blacks' struggles dealing with and overcoming prejudice. I don't think I could really understand what it's like to be Black in this country if I hadn't lived with [Ron] all these years. . . . Even though I'm not African American, it's almost like experiencing it myself.

Although both Greg and Burt come from the dominant U.S. group, because they have access to minority group realities through their partners, they are aware of their privileged position at the same time as they navigate to some extent the culture of their partners.

More than three-quarters of the couples interviewed point to how their identities have changed as a result of both retaining their own cultures (and for some, resisting assimilation to the partner's culture) as well as often simultaneously incorporating some aspects of the other's culture. Thus, acting within their specific social contexts, the people in intercultural partnerships consciously reinvent their identities, becoming increasingly bicultural or multicultural.

Summary and Conclusion

This chapter sheds light on the question why essentialist identities continue to be felt and invoked under presumed conditions of exchange and fluidity, such as when people co-exist on a daily, intimate basis with those who are perceived to come from different cultures. Partners in intercultural relationships recognize cultural identities with distinct boundaries even as those same boundaries are simultaneously shifting and being blurred. Such partners are capable of retaining their cultural identities but also incorporate aspects of their mates' cultures. Thus, couples actively reinvent themselves and develop hybrid relational identities that allow them to function in more than one, and often in at least three, cultural groups or communities.

What this exploration of intercultural couples' identities also shows is that, for the majority, living on a daily basis with someone from another culture leads to respect, understanding, and acceptance of those who are "different." Almost all of the couples included in this study feel enriched by being in an intercultural partnership and appreciate the access and exposure to another world. For most, living with a culturally different partner allows for traveling across cultural boundaries and for gaining new and valuable perspectives on life.

3

Differences That Matter Within Couple Relationships

> [Tony] comes from a very different cultural background than I, but I don't notice it much anymore.... What I do notice is [our] differences regarding finances, how we spend money.... I never had much until I got out of school . . . once you've experienced deprivation, you don't ever want to go back to that again.
>
> —Jessica (European American woman married to a Chinese American man)

The thirty-eight domestic partnerships examined here represent a broad range of ethnic, racial, religious, socioeconomic, and national groups; most also differ by gender. In this and the following chapter, I explore the significance of multiple forms of difference to intercultural couples. How do these social categories vary in their salience and consequences for the couples involved? From the perspective of those living in intergroup partnerships, one may begin to see how their members experience (i.e., are both affected by and resist) the categories of difference commonly used in U.S. society.

This chapter highlights those differences recognized by the couples as most significant *within* their relationships—class and gender—and elucidates the intersection of these categories with ethnicity or culture.

As we will see, class is by far the more important difference and source of conflict for the couples than is gender. This analysis resonates with a number of recent feminist studies of multiple forms of oppression which conclude that "not all differences are created equal" (Ward 2004, 82; see also Glauber 2008; Ollilainen and Calasanti 2007); and that people often feel a sense of greater urgency regarding one or more forms of difference than they do about others (Barvosa-Carter 2001; Calasanti and Slevin 2006; Hurtado 2003; Smith 1993; Takagi 1996). Indeed, in some contexts certain differences may not be relevant at all, while others become particularly salient (Deutsch 2007).

Class

Those who study intergroup couples usually assert that people who form these relationships are typically of the same or similar socioeconomic stratum (Breger and Hill 1998; Diggs 2001; McNamara, Tempanis, and Walton 1999; Root 2001; Spickard 1989). Such studies, however, typically take into consideration the social class of the partners at the time the couples were surveyed or interviewed and do not consider each partner's class of origin, a background factor that may affect profoundly an individual's attitudes regarding material possessions, management of finances, and related issues.[1] Although most of the persons in my sample at the time of their interviews could be placed, based on occupation and education, in the same socioeconomic category as their partners, more than half came from different social class locations and experiences than their partners. Fifty-five percent of the couples admitted to differing attitudes toward money,[2] material possessions, and/or social mobility, and linked the differences to their divergent socioeconomic backgrounds. Many of these couples also connected socioeconomic issues affecting their relationships to the different cultures within which the partners were raised.

Leila (East European American, Jewish) and James (Mexican American, nonpracticing Catholic) were solidly upper middle class at the time of their interviews. Each has a graduate degree and works in a professional occupation earning a comfortable salary—she as a marketing director for a small business, he as a social worker in a large hospital. However, James was born and lived until he was eighteen years old in a poor family and

Differences Within Relationships

neighborhood of a large southwestern city and then subsisted on meager stipends while in college and graduate school. Leila grew up in a well-to-do family in a city on the East Coast with all her material needs met and more. Married twenty-two years, both partners have been acutely aware of these economic differences throughout their lives together.

LEILA: He was just so impoverished when I met him [in graduate school] that he just didn't have anything. . . . His resources were extremely limited and so were his possessions. . . . And so immediately, that was something that was apparent, that was tangible. . . . [Later in their relationship] the thing I always had to remember—and constantly remind myself [of]—is that his frame of reference was so utterly different from mine. . . . That he didn't ever aspire to the kinds of things that I aspired to simply because he thought if you had grass in front of your house you were rich. . . . His rich aunt had grass in front of her house and he had mud. Whereas I grew up in a world where the difference was my friends were going to Europe and I wasn't.

JAMES: I grew up lower class, . . . probably would fit the definition of poverty stricken. . . . The classic matriarchal lower-class existence. Mom with boyfriends, on welfare . . . with no real long-term male figure from beginning to end. . . . The real difference [between him and Leila] was economic.

This couple agrees that their class differences led to differing attitudes and expectations regarding material needs and money and that these divergent attitudes and expectations became the most important source of conflict.

LEILA: So those [economic] kinds of differences simply became more pronounced because as we grew and our family grew and the demands on our resources increased, his satisfaction level was different from mine because I was still perhaps [expecting] more opportunity, more experience, where[as] he was satisfied with experiencing a narrower niche. . . . My needs for security and feeling settled and safe where I know we can sustain a comfortable life are much greater than his ... because he feels incredibly secure in relative terms to what he grew up with. I'm more worried about planning for retirement, ... about how we're going to pay for [the children's] college education, ... about all those middle-class values that were never instilled in him. So as far as he's concerned, we'll always make our way. Whereas I'm always preparing, strategizing, and posturing about what are we going to do to prepare for the future.

JAMES: We started to have serious arguments a few years into our marriage. One day I realized ... this is ridiculous, we're fighting an awful lot. And I thought about it ... let's look at the last five conflicts that [we] had. And every single one of them had a financial basis to it. ... And basically it was my irresponsibility with money, my complete and total lack of any kind of understanding of what money was about. [The way] I grew up—money was simply there to spend. You get it in your pocket, if it was there—'cause you didn't have it very often—and so when you had it, you just spent it. ... Money was a real secondary thing for me. The only time I would save it is when I wanted to buy my mother a Christmas gift. ... And that was the only significance I ever put on money, a way of showing somebody that you really care about them. And other than that, you just spend it when you've got it. [Leila], on the other hand, [has] a completely different approach. You save it. ... I used to kid with her, you save it, you cuddle it, you kiss it, ... you make it grow and then it takes care of you. ... I never looked at it that way. And it spawned these incredible arguments. And it was anything dealing with financial responsibility—saving money, keeping the checkbook, following up on correspondence with insurance—I mean everything financial.

Although this couple dealt with the conflict over finances by agreeing that Leila would be responsible for managing both partners' money, the differences in their attitudes regarding financial security persists and continues to affect the relationship. Although James is resigned that "it's the basic way I am and the basic way she is, and if we're going to act the way we are, that's always going to result in conflict, at least in that area," for Leila, this difference causes considerable hardship and some dissatisfaction with the marriage.

> LEILA: Being married to [James] has complicated my life in some ways.... The fact is that he and I are less compatible over time in terms of our interests and in terms of our pastimes ... going to the symphony, going to the opera, to museums, traveling worldwide ... these are things I fully expected to share in my adulthood.... I'm probably frustrated regarding a lot of the things that I had valued in my life that are ... a part of who I am but I never seem to get enough of.

The couple also perceives their class differences to be related to dissimilar cultural backgrounds. Throughout their interviews, as they talked about the differences between them, the partners frequently switched from economic conditions to their respective cultures. For example, when Leila discusses her and James's different needs for material security, she first mentions their divergent socioeconomic backgrounds as the cause of the difference, and then immediately states, "So that's one very significant difference, *because we come from such different cultures* [emphasis mine], ... I was much more future oriented. And all of his focus was on immediate gratification." Later, when relating the different ways that she and James express themselves, Leila says, "I think his temper is a cultural phenomenon ... maybe [it] was having grown up under extremely stressful conditions, ... maybe [it was] just intimidating people so that nobody would mess with him.... But it was certainly not white middle class!"

In his interview, James talks at length about Leila's focus on finances, implying that it was not due strictly to class but also to her Jewish upbringing: "Her culture equip[ped] her better to manage the finances." He also recognizes Leila's approach to child rearing as originating at least partly in her culture: "I know that the culture [Leila] comes from, corporal punishment isn't part of it." However, he also makes a clear distinction between class and ethnicity when talking about how he and Leila communicate with their families of origin (she on a regular basis, he very infrequently).

> JAMES: This is primarily a [class] difference . . . 'cause the Mexican culture is very family oriented. . . . I think for those of us that grow up poverty stricken, I think it disrupts that [family unity]. And I think we [then] try to have that closeness . . . but it's not the same. . . . Maybe it's the uncertainty of existence . . . where's the next meal coming from? And you know there's adversity, but you also know that family is there or that friends are there [when you need them]. It's a different way of being loyal. . . . There isn't the need for the constant nurturance.

This couple thus clearly regards the partners' social class backgrounds as the most important difference between them. Leila and James acknowledge the independent effect of class on their relationship even though they also recognize the intersection of socioeconomic status and cultural influence.

David (U.S.-born Jew who lived for many years in a kibbutz in Israel) and Leslie (Anglo-American Christian who converted to Judaism), whom we have met in chapter 2, had been married sixteen years and were middle class when interviewed. Each has a college degree; Leslie is a middle school teacher and David works as a reporter for a local newspaper. Leslie grew up in a wealthy, urban midwestern family, while David and his parents spent his entire childhood and adolescence in an Israeli kibbutz, living very simply with few material possessions and comforts. The couple first lived in a commune, sharing a household with others for several years. After having their first child, the pair moved back to the town where they had attended college and bought a single-family home. Both partners recognize the significance of the very different economic circumstances in which they grew up. This dissimilarity affects many aspects of the couple's marriage and is the source of most of their disagreements.

> LESLIE: I was worried how we would be able to support a child. . . . I'm the one who is much more concerned about having things that I think we need, that the kids need, or I need. He could live with almost

no material possessions. He's very resourceful—he knows how to make things from scratch and can get by on anything. I grew up with already made things . . . so I guess I kind of feel deprived if I don't have these things and if my kids don't have them. David and his family had very little when he was growing up.

DAVID: She had grown up with a different consciousness about things, about property and money. . . . I'd grown up in a house where—between what we grew there and what my dad grew in the field for experimental stuff—we pretty much had all our fruits and vegetables. . . . [Leslie] grew up in the fifties [in the United States] with the abundance of the fifties. . . . [Her] family [had a] TV and all the modern conveniences. And I grew up with no TV. . . . In Israel we had nothing, maybe occasionally radio. . . . [There is a] large difference in background.

Both partners admit that the most important disagreements in their marriage focus on different material needs that have been shaped by their earlier economic circumstances. David wants to live simply, collectively, to conserve resources, and not to be surrounded by material possessions. Leslie, however, feels "deprived" if she and her children do not have the material things she believes they need. The couple's first big argument was over moving out of the commune and into their own home; another was about buying a television set. In both cases, Leslie's wishes prevailed, although she compromised by agreeing to have their home be "open to others" and restricting their and their children's exposure to television.

Like Leila, David feels somewhat frustrated with his marriage, the disappointment being unable to live more fully according to his nonmaterialistic values.

DAVID: I've always wanted to live in a community. Ever since I came back from Israel and looked at people in their separate houses, it never made sense to me. It still doesn't make sense. . . . I really wasn't happy [about moving out of the commune]. I still . . . think that was a mistake. . . . It hasn't worked out the way I would have hoped.

Differences Within Relationships

Class issues are closely intertwined with cultural ones, here. The Israeli kibbutz culture, seen by David as fostering values of self-sufficiency, collective existence, and resource conservation, clashes with the individualist, materialist, wealthy European American culture that Leslie accepts.

Another middle-class couple whose published narratives I included in the study are Christy, a forty-five-year-old Northern European American Christian, and Ayoub, an Iranian Muslim seven years younger than his partner, who have lived together for ten years. Both partners earned graduate degrees; Christy is a college professor and Ayoub is an engineer employed by a research firm. Christy grew up in an upper-middle-class family and neighborhood in a large west coast city in the United States, while Ayoub comes from a poor town in a Middle Eastern country. Although both partners recognize many cultural differences between them, the most important source of friction stems from their earlier economic differences.

CHRISTY: The biggest conflict we have is over our spending habits. . . . Ayoub is obsessed with saving money . . . [he is] an inveterate bargain hunter . . . and gets very upset with how I spend money. . . . [When I was growing up], my family shopped in "name" stores and valued "quality" products. I was never taught to save or conserve energy and sometimes I would rather sacrifice savings for convenience. . . . I believe in spending money for enjoyment now, rather than saving everything for the future (although I do have savings) (Brown and Farahyar 1994, 184–85).

AYOUB: The most serious disagreement I have with [Christy] is with Americans' consumerist mentality. American society wastes so much compared with other countries. . . . Christy likes to leave water running, lights on, etc., when she could easily remember to turn things off. She also likes to buy a lot of things she doesn't need. For example, she doesn't need to belong to a health club to exercise when she can exercise outdoors in the park. . . . I see her spending a lot of money on clothes . . . when she already has a lot of clothes. I realize that she has her own money, but since we are sharing a life together, and I am trying to save money for both of us . . . I get the feeling that why should I be willing to sacrifice when she isn't? (190).

Like the other two couples discussed above, Christy and Ayoub find their attitudes about finances permeating many aspects of their relationship, including leisure time together. Ayoub indicates that he does not enjoy many of the activities that Christy does, such as going out to eat, going to the movies, or celebrating holidays such as Christmas and Thanksgiving, all of which "require spending a lot of money." Christy admits that she enjoys going out to eat but that Ayoub always wants to have meals at home because he "believe[s] he can prepare better food at home for less money. . . . The only time I can go to a 'quality' restaurant is when I'm attending a conference or have lunch with a friend, because Ayoub refuses to try these restaurants" (181). Because Ayoub does not like to go out to the movies ("When I suggest going to a movie he usually says he prefers to stay at home"), the couple "now . . . rent videos fairly often, which is a fairly acceptable compromise" (190).

Although this couple is able to learn to live with many differences they perceive to be cultural (e.g., food preferences, family relations), their divergent economic orientations continue to strain the relationship. Ayoub claims to have become resigned to Christy's spending habits: "[I] feel that [I] cannot change the person and just g[a]ve up trying and accept her buying whatever she likes, [though he still doesn't like it]" (190). Christy, on the other hand, continues to resent his attitude.

> Ayoub has gradually stopped protesting about everything I buy . . . and I have become more conscious of saving money, but we still have serious differences. I think for me the most serious consequence is when Ayoub objects to my spending money to buy books, to go conferences, or to buy a PC, because these things are connected to my work. I earn enough money to buy these things and should be able to make my own decision about what to buy, and Ayoub cannot really stop me. Thus I have bought everything I need, but Ayoub's objections create a psychological pressure, and I must spent time justifying my purchases (185).

Christy also sees her partner's differing attitude toward finances to be "partly related to culture." She frequently mentions that Ayoub is Middle Eastern or Iranian in his orientation and that his focus on saving and always looking for bargains is a trait among people she has known from that part of the world or that nationality. She also claims, though, that she "realize[s] . . . cultures are going through a process of modernization [and change] affects individuals differently depending on their class [and] their country of origin" (174). And in the case of Ayoub, who was raised in a poor, "peasant" family, "because [he has] this type of background, he has not adopted Western fashions and consumerism as many middle-class Iranians [I have known]" (178). Ayoub in turn attributes Christy's consumerist habits to the mainstream "U.S. western culture" in which she grew up. Both thus perceive the independent effect of class on their attitudes toward economic issues while also acknowledging that class intersects with each partner's cultural heritage.

Many other couples included in this study similarly find background economic differences between them to cause conflict over spending habits and related issues. George (East African from Tanzania) and Nancy (Italian American) have been married six years, are highly educated (both have graduate degrees), and are employed in professional occupations (he as a technology consultant and she as a hospital administrator). Both regard the economic differences of their backgrounds as more important than culture or race.

> GEORGE: I am very careful about where every dollar goes; I think it's because of all the years I had to scrape by on very little. And it's not that she's a reckless spender, . . . but she thinks that we should spend a lot on the children, on whatever they need or want, and I don't think it's so important to buy a lot of toys or clothes. I'd rather save more for their education, but [Nancy] wants them to have things that their friends have so they don't feel deprived.
>
> NANCY: I never wanted for anything when I was growing up, though we weren't rich. . . . So I would like my children to have the things I was able to have. [George] can't understand that because he

had so little in [Africa], so if our kids have some books and toys and clothes, he thinks this is a huge amount of stuff, but it's not more, and probably much less, than most middle-class American kids have. . . . We still have disagreements about spending money on things like Christmas presents. He'll say, "In my culture we don't give presents and it's a waste of money to buy all these things."

Like other couples, many aspects of this pair's existence are seen as affected by the intersection of each partner's class and culture of origin. For instance, George was overly protective of their children when they were infants because, explains Nancy, "The infant mortality rate in [East Africa] is so high. . . . Among all that poverty, he saw children die. . . . His culture places a lot of importance on protecting kids." And George attributes their differing emphases on hard work to class as well as to cultural backgrounds.

GEORGE: I had to work hard ever since I was a child because everybody in [his community] did. . . . We were all taught to work very hard; it was part of the way of life. I still can't sit still for very long without fixing something around the house. [Nancy] is a hard worker, but she knows how to relax, too. She has that middle-class view of leisure I don't have; it comes from the American leisure culture.

Elsa (Swiss-German American from a middle-class background) and Sean (working-class Irish American), both first generation U.S. immigrants who have been married twenty-five years, also recognize economic class differences within their partnership and relate the dissimilarities to essentialist cultural backgrounds.

ELSA: [Sean] grew up in a situation with even less financial security than what we had, certainly, and with much less things. He is happier with much less, in many ways. . . . And that's also because of his Irish outlook; he's just kind of more accepting of things as they come.

Differences Within Relationships

> SEAN: [When] the Irish in me comes out . . . I tend to be very lax; I don't see money as that important. [Elsa], she takes care of our accounts. She is very, very organized. . . . She keeps the office—we have a home office—in order. . . . The Swiss, very much like Germans, [see that] everything has a place. She pays attention to the details.

Myra (French Canadian from a working-class family) and Peter (Hungarian American from a poor peasant background), married thirty-two years, likewise are very aware of their economic differences and see them as closely tied to their different cultures.

> MYRA: I came from a family—we didn't have much—but there were gifts for kids [at holidays] and I used to love to spend for them. . . . People in our whole [French Canadian] community would celebrate and go all out for the holidays. And he came from poverty and wasn't brought up in a place where they spent a lot for the kids . . . he thought spending money like this was a waste.

Peter had very few material resources growing up on an impoverished farm in Hungary. During the Second World War he was taken at the age of fourteen to a work camp in Germany—and managed to survive despite deplorable conditions. He returned to Hungary after the war, but left the country during the 1956 uprising and found his way to the United States. Experiences of deprivation and trauma left him wanting material security. Peter also asserts that in the Hungarian peasant culture "people didn't give each other presents" and that holiday celebrations include "lots of drinking and dancing, but you didn't buy things for your wife or kids." This couple perceives both class and cultural backgrounds to be responsible for shaping their attitudes toward money and spending habits.

Not all of the couples in this study who come from dissimilar socioeconomic circumstances recognize intersections of class and culture. Ron, an African American accountant, and Greg, an Irish American graphic designer, have lived together for ten years. Ron grew up poor in the rural U.S. South and Greg came from a well-to-do urban east

Differences Within Relationships

coast family. Financial issues continue to be a major source of conflict for this couple.

> RON: We disagree about spending money. [Greg] spends more than I do; I'm much more careful. I think this comes from having grown up in poverty. [Greg] grew up comfortably; his family was pretty solid middle class, maybe upper class. He never had to live hand to mouth. We have separate bank accounts, but still I'm concerned that he doesn't save for a rainy day.

> GREG: I'm kind of loose with money and I think that comes from privilege, from being around wealth. [Ron]'s attitude to money is different . . . he's really tight when it comes to money. He came from poverty and always reminds me that he worked very hard for everything he has.

Although Ron and Greg also acknowledge cultural differences between them, they do not think they are as important as the dissimilarities stemming from early economic circumstances and they do not connect class with their cultures of origin.

Jessica (European American) and Tony (Chinese American), married seventeen years, were middle class at the time of their interviews. Jessica owns and manages a small business, Tony is a successful landscape design artist, and each of the partners takes home a relatively large paycheck. Jessica comes from a midwestern working-class background, while Tony grew up in a wealthy Asian American family on the West Coast. As Jessica's interview excerpt in the beginning of this chapter indicates, she no longer notices the cultural differences between herself and Tony. What she does notice is the partners' different attitudes about managing finances and spending habits.

> JESSICA: I am very careful about how I spend money and I just get so frustrated when I see [Tony] buying things we really don't need. . . . I never had much until I got out of school and started my own business. I sometimes feel I should be able to let go, to spend freely and enjoy myself, but there's always that voice inside my head saying "you shouldn't spend it; save it."

TONY: We've never had disagreements about the cultural things. What we argue about is money, which is absurd because we both make enough so that we can live well and save, too. It's mainly about my spending more than she does and her wanting to save everything. I realize that she had so little when she was growing up and I was advantaged, I didn't have to work and go to school at the same time, so I understand that she feels financially insecure, no matter how much we have.

Another couple with different socioeconomic backgrounds is John, a European-American Christian from a middle-class Southern family, and Amy, a first-generation immigrant from Switzerland from a working-class Jewish family. Married for twenty-six years, they have this to say about their class and cultural differences:

JOHN: The cultural differences [between us] I don't think were really very significant.... Her background had been one of a lot of deprivation. So her aggressiveness to get what she wanted and needed for herself was different than mine. Mine was a much more sheltered and nurtured, economically well-off background,... so I was probably less... demanding about things because it's no big deal to get what I wanted.

AMY: Even though we come from very different backgrounds, the cultural differences have never been that important.... What's been more important in our marriage is that he's always lived a very comfortable life, and I had to work very hard when I was growing up and until we met, and even now I'm always working much harder than he is.... He doesn't really understand my drive, my desire to have things and to live life fully.

Silvia (Peruvian) and Bill (English Canadian transplanted to the United States), married twenty-three years, are similarly aware of economic differences without connecting them to their disparate cultural backgrounds.

BILL: I don't have a good concept of money... maybe [because of] my background.... I was brought up very poor.... We ate because the lady at the store gave us the food 'til my father got paid,... 'cause my mother died when I was very young... and I had to work and go to school.... I never worried about finances—[when he and Silvia] first got married I had no money and we led a good life. But I tend to be careless and [Silvia] is more conservative.

SILVIA: [Bill] doesn't pay attention to money, but I watch what we spend.... I learned from my mother [who was the president of a food cooperative] to be careful and to try to save.... So we argue about money sometimes.

For Ron and Greg, Jessica and Tony, John and Amy, Myra and Peter, Silvia and Bill, the partners' divergent economic backgrounds constitute the most salient difference to be dealt with inside the couple relationship. In all five cases, however, unlike the other couples discussed in this chapter, these partners do not perceive the behaviors and attitudes related to their class of origin to also be connected to culture.

Looking at the class issue from another angle, although it might be expected that cultural differences are likely to be more salient for couples where the partners' class backgrounds are similar, this is not a finding of the study. Although couples with partners of the same or similar class background recognize cultural differences, they do not see their different cultures to be a consistently salient feature of their relationships. For example, Roy (African American/American Indian) and Lee (Chinese American), both from working-class families and having lived together for five years, pay little attention to their cultural differences. As Roy observes, "Even though Lee and I come from very different cultures, it doesn't seem to matter." Lee admits, "I'm surprised sometimes that we don't notice the differences more.... As a couple, Roy and I don't dwell on the different cultural aspects." Likewise, Linda (European American) and Kishan (East Asian Indian) both from middle-class families, agree that cultural differences are not very important to their marriage.

LINDA: It amazes me that we don't have more differences than we do.

KISHAN: Despite initially seeing the differences, as we've settled into our marriage, the cultural things don't seem to matter any more.

In sum, for more than half of the couples in this study, early economic circumstances constitute the most significant difference in their relationships. Even though many perceive economic class to be related to culture or ethnicity, in their views, class of origin independently affects attitudes and behavior related to spending habits and other financial and material aspects of the relationships. As the above examples show, usually—although not in every case—the partner from a lower- or working-class background is more concerned about the couple's financial situation than the partner who grew up middle or upper class. Moreover, the differing attitudes and orientations of partners toward financial matters cause most of the disagreements between them and are often the source of at least some dissatisfaction with the relationship.

Ethnicity or national cultural heritage is sometimes perceived by the couples to bear some relationship to economic class background and the resulting attitudes and behaviors regarding financial matters. The vast majority (90 percent) of the couples with partners of different social class backgrounds, however, do not view their cultural differences to be as significant as those of class.

Gender

Like economic class, gender (identity and behavior rooted in notions of femininity and masculinity) affects the couples' relationships in a variety of ways, and is often perceived to be related to culture, class, and race. For instance, as I indicated in chapter 2, white European-American middle- and upper-class males are more likely than dominant group females to be aware of a couple's cultural differences. The dominant group male partners, in a privileged position, tend to overlook cultural differences and to take their cultural identity for granted.

Differences Within Relationships

The gender differences that the heterosexual couples in this study particularly recognize as most salient are those related to "sex/gender roles"—the appropriate expectations for women and men in domestic partnerships. In many cases, especially among the international heterosexual couples, the partners' divergent views of these expectations are attributed to differences in cultures.

Nancy (Italian American), married for six years to George (East African), is keenly aware of the gender roles in her spouse's culture that differ greatly from her views (which she sees as being "influenced by the U.S. feminist movement") of appropriate behavior for women and men.

> NANCY: For me, a lot of [the cultural differences between us] are tied to the status of women in terms of what the traditional roles of women ... and men are, what traditional family roles are in [George's] culture.... There's an idea that women do the cooking—men don't cook. For instance, there's a corn flour kind of porridge ... that's a very basic, staple food and it's something that women make and little girls learn how to make, and [although] everyone knows how to make it, men don't make it. When they're living alone they will make it but as soon as a woman comes into their life it's the woman's job to do that. I refused to make it for years because it was the mark of: "No, I'm not entering into that system. You know how to make it and if you want [to eat] it, you make it."

George also is well aware of these cultural expectations and of their influence on his behavior.

In [Tanzania] there are very distinct roles for men and women. Women are supposed to do all the cooking, taking care of children, cleaning houses, as well as doing things like gardening and farming. Men are supposed to work to support the family, and to do any of the women's work is considered shameful.... Although I didn't stick to the traditional male role as much as most men, I have to admit that when [Nancy] was staying home [after their first child was born] it was very easy for me to expect her to do most of the cooking, housework, and childcare.

Although both partners recognize their differing views concerning gender roles and also realize that these expectations are shaped by the societies in which they had lived, nevertheless in practice the division of labor between them in the household varies depending on the circumstances. For instance, though George often cooked when the couple was first married, when their African friends came to dinner, the couple would pretend that Nancy had prepared the food.

> NANCY: He would do virtually all the cooking, but ahead of time so that when [African friends] came over, I was the one in the kitchen as if I was the one who made all the food. He would say that if people knew he'd made it, they wouldn't eat it. If a man makes it, it doesn't taste good. I would say that that's absolutely ridiculous, . . . but I'd compromise and be in the kitchen when people arrived.

When Nancy stayed home with their firstborn, the couple fell into a more traditional pattern; Nancy did most of the cooking and childcare. The partners' roles switched when Nancy obtained a permanent job and George began temporarily working part time.

> GEORGE: Once [Nancy] got her job, it all changed. Actually, I was the one then without a steady income and she was mostly supporting the family. So, in fact, for a while the roles were reversed. I did all the housework and childcare then.

Eventually, the couple started sharing responsibilities more equally. As Nancy states, "We both now have full-time jobs and pretty much share all the household tasks. We take turns cooking, and we both take care of the children, shop for groceries, clean the house." George concurs. "Now, after six years of marriage, I think we are at a point where we are pretty equal partners."

Christy (Northern-European American, Christian) and Ayoub (Iranian Muslim) similarly are cognizant of how culturally gendered roles influence their relationship.

Differences Within Relationships

CHRISTY: In many ways Ayoub is more open and flexible than some Middle Eastern men I had met.... [He accepts] women's right to work and believes in sharing of housework.... He believe[s] women should work because staying at home would be frustrating and would limit one's growth as a person.... (Brown and Farhayar 1994, 178).... But he still tends to tell me what to do. I think Ayoub's tendency to try to make decisions for me is more or less unconscious; it's the way he was brought up and it's very hard to change (184).

Ayoub points out that in his culture gender roles are very traditional and that there are generally clearly separate worlds for women and men. However, by the time he met Christy his ideas about gender changed. "I developed my ideas about men's and women's sexual equality from the leftist groups who saw women in Iran as oppressed but also saw Western women as treated as sex objects and not truly liberated" (187). Thus, over time, Ayoub came to no longer accept "the double standard for men and women." He is aware though that sometimes he slips because those traditional views are still deeply ingrained (ibid).

Within this ten-year relationship, Ayoub does most of the cooking and grocery shopping and shares with his partner other household tasks. He was also very supportive of Christy's career as a college professor, including during an extended period of time when he was unemployed and searched for a job after obtaining his graduate degree. Although aware of culturally gendered roles, in most ways this couple does not exhibit traditional gender relations and does not perceive gender differences to be a particularly salient feature of their partnership.

Married fifteen years, Isabela (Chilean) and Graham (Irish American) do not adhere to traditional gender expectations although both are from cultural backgrounds where women were assumed to be the ones to stay home while men supported the family.

ISABELA: In [Chile] women are very attentive to their husbands.... They'd be like, "Honey, would you like some coffee?" "Honey would you like this? Would you like that?" And [Graham] knows I don't cook . . . there are a lot of things [around the house] that I don't do. . . . And there are a lot of pressures for being in that kind of atmosphere [conform to traditional roles for women], for being like a [Chilean].

GRAHAM: I'm kind of like the old school. I grew up with my mom taking care of us and dad going to work. He never did any housework or anything. I believe a woman should cook. And [Isabela] doesn't cook at all. So I do all the cooking and I spend a lot of time with the children. I took care of them a lot when they were small.

Graham also supported Isabela's decision to go to college and then to take a demanding job as a publicist for a large business firm. Like most of the other international couples in the study, this pair, although exposed for much of their lives to traditional gender roles, do not conform to them within their relationship.

Domestic (U.S.-born) partners often view gender differences as independent of their cultural, and sometimes economic, backgrounds. For instance, Carlie (African-American Christian) and Gary (Jewish American of East European heritage), married twenty-one years, have this to say about gender in their relationship:

GARY: The past twenty years have revealed gender and class as bigger issues than race in our marriage. . . . When we have disagreements about how to spend money, how and where to save it, this [is related to class differences]. I grew up with financial security and she did not. . . . I am much more interested in buying things than Carlie [is]. . . . She, on the other hand, will spend more freely on clothes than I will, . . . while it was I who pushed for a new sound system and . . . a computer. . . . A good deal of this is certainly a matter of gender. (Tartakov and Tartakov 1994, 151)

Carlie concurs that race and ethnicity have a lesser effect on the couples' relationship "than class and perceptions of sex roles" (130). She also states emphatically that she and Gary have worked throughout their marriage to make the relationship as equal as possible:

Differences Within Relationships

The major characteristic of this marriage has been its equality and sharing. We have from the beginning, both felt willing to do whatever needed doing.... We've shared household work and the children, career development and friends, in a continually satisfying way. And when one can't get there to make an appointment, or can't cook, because something has come up, the other takes over (150).

Similarly, Leila (East European-American Jew) and James (Mexican American, nonpracticing Catholic), who see some gender differences in their relationship that are independent of their specific cultural backgrounds, also emphasize gender equality.

JAMES: Early on, when the kids were little, there definitely was a difference that emerged in the roles that we took on. And it was pretty traditional.... I was the disciplinarian, the authority [figure], and [Leila] was the nurturing one. I don't think this was cultural—just the usual gender stuff—and I don't know how that happened because we went into this as a real partnership.... When the girls got older, our [parenting] roles were not that different. Leila and I both dealt with discipline and I became more nurturing. And that was the only significant gender difference that we had.... From the start of our relationship I did everything around the apartment.... I cleaned it, did the laundry, did the dishes... because it was fair.... And I still do a lot around the house.

LEILA: I think [James] has always been subtly sexist simply because, growing up as a male [in the United States], I think he viewed women in some respects as sex objects.... And there are always the jokes and the little quips and remarks about my chest, but that's not really on a serious level.... I think that in terms of gender roles, he was already liberated by the time I met him. He would do dishes, clean the house, he always did the laundry. And he never imposed his will on me in terms of my career aspirations, my personal relationships. I've never asked his approval of anything. I've wanted his agreement because I respect his opinion, but if I feel strongly that I need to do something, he would never stand in my way. We have such mutual respect for each other that we never stand in each other's way in any fashion.

Jessica (European American) and Tony (Chinese American) describe the significance of gender differences in their relationship and do not attribute them to their different cultural backgrounds.

JESSICA: I don't notice the cultural differences.... I think we differ on some issues because I see things differently as a woman and he as a man. So I pay more attention to detail, like what the house looks like, decorating it and such. And he kind of takes that for granted. And I pay more attention to clothes and how I look.

TONY: We joke sometimes about how, even though I'm a [landscape] designer, I don't pay attention to things in the house, but I notice every detail when I'm working on someone's yard. I'm just not as oriented to making a house look nice as she is. But that's not a cultural difference—that's a gender difference.

This couple shares all housework and childcare responsibilities, and makes joint decisions.

JESSICA: We try to divide up everything equally. The one thing I hate doing is laundry, and since he doesn't mind it, he does most of that. Otherwise, we both cook and clean, and whoever has time buys groceries. We both take care of [their daughter]. He always did his share with her, changed her diapers, took her for walks, read to her—everything.... We make all decisions together, about jobs and bigger purchases, and anything regarding [their daughter].

TONY: We pretty much share all the work in the house.... When it comes to making decisions for each of us and as a family, we make them together.

In almost all of the intercultural couples, the international and U.S. heterosexual partners defy traditional gender prescriptions. Although most have struggled at some points in their relationships with gendered patterns of behavior, there is typically a great deal of sharing of responsibilities and decision making between the partners. Men and women together perform traditionally female tasks in households, such as cooking, cleaning, and childcare; in some instances, even though the couples strive to share equally, the men do more of these tasks, especially cooking, than the women. These couples thus appear more egalitarian than those in the general U.S. population, where most women, though they typically work outside the home, still do the majority of household and childcare labor while men usually "help" (Bianchi et al. 2000; Coltrane 2000; National Survey of Families and Households 2005).

The same-sex couples in this study show an even greater tendency toward equal sharing of domestic responsibilities than the heterosexual couples. The partners often talk about sharing household tasks fifty-fifty, and filling in for each other when the need arises. For example, Mae (African American) and Penny (Irish American), who have lived together for five years, state,

> PENNY: We do all of the household chores together, or sometimes take turns, depending on who's got more time. If it's my turn to cook and something comes up, then Mae will do it, if she can. Then the next day, I'll cook. Often we just cook together.
>
> MAE: We share everything equally except the laundry. Penny does the laundry because she knows if I do it, then some of the clothes will be shrunk.

Claudia (Brazilian) and Stephanie (Scandinavian American), who have been together ten years, also practice an egalitarian division of household labor.

> CLAUDIA: [Steph] and I share all the housework. Sometimes, she may cook more and at other times I do; it depends on what's happening with our jobs, when one of us may have to work lon-

Differences Within Relationships

ger hours.... We clean the house together, although I'm not as neat as she is, and we each do our own laundry.

STEPHANIE: We both like to cook, so we take turns or sometimes cook together. [Claudia] hates to clean and I don't mind it, so I do more of that.... We share shopping and laundry fifty-fifty.

Ron (African American/Indian American) and Greg (Irish American), together for almost ten years, have this to say.

RON: We both do what needs to be done. We share equally the cleaning and shopping, the laundry. I do more of the cooking, but that's because I'm just better at it.

GREG: We try to do most things equally. [Ron's] a better cook than I, and he likes to cook, so he does most of the cooking. Otherwise, we share everything fifty-fifty.

And Lee (Chinese American) and Roy (of African American and American Indian ancestry), who have lived together five years, say:

LEE: We make a real effort to divide all [housework] equally.... We don't like to do most of it, so it's easier to have two people share the work and it gets done quicker. We clean our condo about every two to three weeks and we often go grocery shopping together and we cook together, when we cook. Most of the time we're so busy that we eat out or pick up prepared food from a deli.

ROY: All the household tasks are definitely shared equally by us. I'd say it's a fifty-fifty division, neither of us does more or less of anything.

The even more equal sharing of household tasks among intergroup, same-sex couples than among the heterosexual domestic partnerships in this study is consistent with previous research that finds egalitarian division of labor to be much more common among lesbian and gay couples than among heterosexual pairs (Blumstein and Schwartz 1983; Coontz 2008; Kurdek and Schmitt 1987; Patterson 1995; Peplau and Spalding 2000).

What may be the reasons for the intercultural couples as a group to exhibit more egalitarianism and gender role flexibility than couples in the general population? Some clues come from several of the heterosexual partners, who claim that had they been in a relationship with a person from their own culture, they would have been more likely to acquiesce to traditional gender expectations. For instance, Ayoub, Christy's partner, claims,

> If I had married an Iranian woman, even a professional woman, she would automatically cook and take care of the house (although I would help her). She would probably be more sexually conservative than most American women, but she would probably want to have children immediately, and she would be very close to her family (Brown and Farahyar 1994, 189).

Christy, who was married for several years to a man from a culture more similar to her own (European American) before she met Ayoub, recalls the relationship as very traditional. "I did all the cooking and most of the housework, and when my husband went to the grocery store with me he complained that he was bored and had no idea what we should buy; he got mad at me if I lost one of his socks" (185). Ayoub's and Christy's intercultural relationship is a dramatic departure from what each expected or experienced in long-term relationships with partners from their respective cultural groups.

Similarly, Suzy (Japanese American) married to Russell (Polish American), notes,

> If I'd married a man from my own culture, I think [the marriage] might be more traditional.... I have Japanese American friends, women who married men from their [own] culture and they're not employed; they stay home with the kids and their husbands support them.

Russell likewise experienced traditional gender roles in a brief relationship with a Polish American woman.

Differences Within Relationships

She wanted me to do things that men traditionally did: to open doors for her, to order for her in restaurants. She wouldn't let me do anything around the apartment, didn't want me near the kitchen. And it was easy to go along with that.

Tony (Chinese American) and Jessica (European American) also had similar experiences before they met.

> TONY: I lived for a while with a girl who was Chinese. She treated me like some sort of a king. I'm ashamed to say that she waited on me hand and foot. But that got really old after a while.
>
> JESSICA: Before I got involved with Tony, I had several relationships with guys who were closer to my own background. These relationships were more traditional. A couple of the men were very controlling and I had to keep asking them to help me clean up and such.

How do the intercultural couples explain why their relationships are so much more egalitarian than the ones they had or would expect to have had within their own cultural groups? Ayoub suggests that if he were married to an Iranian woman their shared culture would make it difficult to break out of traditional roles, as there would be pressures, especially from family, to follow customs that others in the culture accept. On the other hand, being in a cross-cultural relationship, "we both have been able to adapt to each other's cultures [in order to] get along" (Brown and Farahyar 1994, 191).

Similarly, Suzy states:

> I would try to work [if married to a Japanese American man]. But his family might pressure me to stay at home, and if we lived in a neighborhood with other Japanese [families], it would be much harder for me to do what I'd want. Since we are away from both our families and have been able to make an independent life ourselves, it is much easier for us to lead our lives the way we decide. Being away from my culture and in an intercultural relationship has made it more possible for me to put into practice my ideals of how women and men should live together.

Suzy's spouse, Russell, indicates:

> I think being in an intercultural marriage, it's like you're not quite in one culture or the other, so both [Suzy] and I have the freedom to take from our cultures, our backgrounds, those aspects that we want, and not to accept those things we don't [want] and to build something new.... I was much more aware in my relationship with her, from the beginning, that it would be different than those I've had before. So, it just couldn't be a traditional relationship; it had to be a relationship between two equals making a life together out of two, no, three cultures.

And Tony explains:

> Even though younger [Chinese] Americans are not as traditional as their parents, there is still this strong emphasis on male children, the heirs to the family fortune, the ones who are to take care of parents when they get old. So men have a lot of privileges. Usually people [Chinese Americans] aren't even aware of this, but once they step out of that culture, once they live with someone who is different, and can look at it more objectively, they realize that it's not such a great system. So I think being in an intercultural relationship gave me more awareness, a different perspective on gender issues.

These partners thus attribute the relative gender equality in their relationships to the more fluid context of intercultural relationships in which neither partner is expected to conform to traditional precepts, and where together they are able to consciously create a union that may not fit the prescriptions of either culture. Since an intergroup domestic partnership already defies social norms by crossing the boundaries of ethnicity, race, and/or nationality, it is likely also to defy traditional gender expectations.

Because the heterosexual couples in this study have achieved a high level of gender equality, gender differences are not a particularly salient feature of their relationships. If gender differences are perceived to exist, especially in regard to tasks performed within the household, this occurred usually in the early stages of relationships; in most cases, the couples over time develop a relatively egalitarian division of labor, and gender becomes an increasingly less important difference. For same-sex couples, no gender differences regarding household division of labor were found between the lesbian and gay couples. All six same-sex pairs appear to have a similarly high level of equality between the partners.

Summary and Conclusion

Class difference is a significantly more salient issue within intercultural domestic partnerships than is gender. The couples are able to negotiate gender role differences much more effectively than the attitudes and practices stemming from divergent socioeconomic backgrounds. Although many of the couples perceive both class and gender to be related to culture of origin, they do not make direct linkages between class and gender. Thus, while growing up in poverty or coming from lower, working, or middle class are often mentioned as possible reasons for attitudes toward finances and related issues, class status is absent from accounts of couple partners' views regarding expectations of males and females.

For the couples in this study, gender differences are clearly "negotiable," while economic differences are seen as highly problematic and requiring special strategies to manage. (I discuss this at some length in chapter 5.) The partners can supply a rationale for why their relationships are relatively egalitarian in terms of gender, but they typically are not able to account for why they could not resolve the problems attributable to class differences. In most cases where differences between the partners in class background exist, economic issues are a source of ongoing conflict that negatively affects the quality of the relationship.

In *Where We Stand: Class Matters* (2000), bell hooks points out that although in the United States we have been engaging for some time in a public dialogue about gender and race, "as a nation we are afraid to have a dialogue about class" (vii). According to hooks, the binary categories typically used to conceive of race (black/white) and gender (male/female) are nonexistent when it comes to class, which takes on many complex dimensions in a global capitalist system. Because we are less conscious of how class affects our lives and lack the concepts and language to critique and change class relations, our struggles around class remain superficial at best. Hence, "the closest most folks can come to talking about class in this nation is to talk about money" (5). The couples I interviewed do indeed focus on money issues as a primary way to talk about class and they are typically at a loss when dealing with the effects of their economic background differences. On the other hand, the partners are quite adept in discussing gendered roles and their conscious practices in building egalitarian gender relationships. However, the intergroup nature of these couples' relationships gives them perspectives that make the partners more "sensitive" to social differences than the average person living in the United States and thus more likely to acknowledge that class, gender, and related cultural differences matter inside their unions. Although the couples may have lacked the "tools" to effectively resolve the problems stemming from class differences, they are, nevertheless, quite aware of the role of divergent socioeconomic status within their relationships.

4

Differences That Matter Across Relationships

> Inside the marriage we relate as an ordinary couple. . . . Clearly, society notices and attaches much more importance to the interracial . . . character of our relationship than we do. These are minor attributes for us, but for others, they are often the only attributes (Johnson and Johnson 1994, 199–200).
>
> —Walton (African American man married to a British woman)

Let's now turn our attention to a different set of differences, those less salient to the partners as a couple but mattering more to those external to the union—persons with whom the partners have invested outside relationships (extended family members, friends, co-workers, neighbors) as well as total strangers.[1]

The categories of difference that outsiders consider most salient, according to the intercultural couples' reports, are those of race and religion. Although these differences are of little perceived importance to the partners within the couple relationship, in dealing with the outside world interracial couples in particular recount incidents of racism and discrimination. Those in interfaith partnerships in some cases experience pressure or even outright rejection from family members.

Interracial same-sex couples, in addition to being made aware of their race differences by outsiders, are simultaneously the victims of homophobic attitudes and behaviors.

Race

Interracial relationships have been subject to grave social sanctions in American society. Marriage between Blacks and Whites was illegal in many states until relatively recently (McNamara, Tempenis, and Walton 1999, 21–22) and, even today, many interracial couples are not accepted by their families and may be treated with hostility or disdain by strangers (Childs 2005).[2] However, for the interracial couples in this study (58 percent of the sample), race differences, although typically recognized as significant at the beginning of relationships, diminished greatly in importance once the partners became a committed couple.

In chapter 2, I noted that partners in several interracial couples were hesitant at first to form intimate relationships with someone of a different race. George (Tanzanian) and Nancy (Italian American) saw each other socially for almost a year before they became "serious." Adida (South African) and Steven (American of German extraction) knew each other for four years before marrying, having dated on and off for about two years. Linda (European American) and Kishan (East Asian Indian) were friends for a year before they started a romantic relationship. Mae (African American) and Penny (Irish American) admit that they were reluctant to acknowledge the attraction they felt for one another due in large part to race differences. Suzy (Asian American of Japanese descent) and Russell (Polish American) recall that their relationship developed very slowly because both were apprehensive about becoming involved with a person from a different racial group.

Once the partners realized that they had romantic feelings for each other and that they wanted to be together, race was no longer a barrier. In fact, it seemed to retreat from immediate awareness, resurfacing only when reminded by others outside the relationship. George and Nancy have this to say about the interracial aspects of their relationship.

Differences Across Relationships

GEORGE: I remember before I was first attracted to [Nancy], thinking how light her skin was. Now... it seems really silly and unreal, because it no longer matters.... As we got to know each other better ....the skin color thing receded into the background somewhere. More important were things like her personality and her warmth,... understanding.

NANCY: [At first] there was my reticence about the fact that [George] was from a different race. I remember telling [an African female friend], "He's so dark! If he was more your color it wouldn't be such a shock to me." She said, "Well, you know, we come in all different colors." I remember going to a picnic that first spring when we really started going out.... When I first got there I was the only white person there.... I remember being very conscious of that fact. And I remember that because, in contrast,... around [the] time of our wedding—there's one picture in our wedding album that's all the [Africans] and [George] and me. I looked at that picture several times and then one day I realized that when I look at that picture I don't see any difference between me and anybody else. It's not true that I'm colorblind.... It's just sort of, "now you're among people [you] know," and I feel very comfortable in a group of Africans.... Now I don't even notice it [race].

The couple acknowledges, however, that there are times when they are reminded of race.

GEORGE: There are sometimes situations where we are made aware of our race difference, like when we go to a restaurant or some place like that, and are the only couple or family that is mixed, or when everybody else is white.

NANCY: We went [to a function] recently and there was a little girl playing outside and [pointing to their daughter]. She said, "Did you have her or did you adopt her?" People often ask me questions like that.... Sometimes it's a painful question because, you know, obviously [she] is. "Can't you tell this is my daughter?"

[113]

Nancy remembers a relative of hers who made her and George feel very uncomfortable by telling racist and sexist jokes. The couple tried not to react, but Nancy did finally say that she did not appreciate the humor. She was hurt and unhappy about the incident. Nancy also confesses that "we have encountered some hostility from African Americans . . . about the fact that we have a biracial relationship." Being in an interracial relationship also has made Nancy more sensitive to race in public situations. "We went somewhere the other day, maybe McDonald's . . . and I'm always conscious now, and I never used to be, of looking around me and thinking, 'Oh, there are only white people here.' That's something that never bothered me before [she was with George]."

Nevertheless, despite the racism of outsiders and the heightened awareness of their difference in the public sphere by the white partner, for this couple race has no perceived effect on the quality of their relationship.

> GEORGE: For us, as a couple, as a family, race is not important. [Calling attention to race by outsiders] is a relatively minor thing, as we are a strong couple together and don't let it bother us.

> NANCY: In some ways people [may] think our marriage is very difficult. When people . . . look at us they [tend to] think that problems we might have as a family would be related to the fact that we are of two different races, when in my mind that really doesn't enter into our relationship all that much.

Although they do not see race as a salient factor inside their four-year marriage, Adida (Black South African) and Steven (White American of German heritage) nevertheless confronted Steven's parents' prejudice against Adida.

> ADIDA: It [race] became an issue when his parents started knowing that we [were] dating. . . . His parents were opposed to the relationship. . . . And I think I became more conscious of race after this than I have ever been in my life . . . because of the way his parents reacted.

STEVEN: My family has been contentious.... They haven't been supportive or accepting of [Adida] and I lament it, ... and sometimes it's easier to deal with than [at] other [times].

Steven's parents did not attend the couple's wedding and wanted nothing to do with Adida until the couple's child was born, at which point they came to see their grandson. But they still do not accept Adida as a family member. The parents' rejection of their son's spouse puts a great strain on Steven's relationship with them but it does not affect the marriage.

ADIDA: It doesn't really matter whether the person is of a different race or a different ethnic group or a different religion, people always come up with these differences, and if they take them seriously, then it can be an issue, and people can go as far as killing each other for those things. I think that [realization] helped me really develop the sense that it doesn't matter how everybody else feels. This is how I feel... and I'm going to stand for what I feel and what I think is right. We didn't intend to hurt the parents.... [Steven] feels the same way, and together we are able to put the problem with his parents out of our lives most of the time.

STEVEN: I think that the problem with my parents, and how we've dealt with it, has strengthened our marriage. We have created a kind of common front and don't let the issue intrude into our marriage. Race may be an issue for them, but it's not for us.

Patsy (Asian, Filipina) and Don (African American), one of the couples featured in chapter 1, despite some initial apprehension—especially on Patsy's part—likewise do not regard race as a significant factor in their fourteen-year marriage. At first Patsy refused to go out with Don because of her own prejudice against Blacks ("I was always friendly to foreigners but not a black man!") and her fear that her reputation would be destroyed if she dated Don ("It would [be] the same as [being] a prostitute ... I did not want to be identified with a black man."). Although Don

Differences Across Relationships

claims that Patsy being Asian was not an initial barrier for him, he admits being aware of the stereotype of the Westerner desiring a submissive Oriental "and then, on the other hand, the African American stereotyped male [being] more virile and all that." Over time, as the partners became better acquainted, Patsy realized that Don was "so nice and educated and [getting to know him] erased this misconception" she had of Blacks. And Don discovered that Patsy defied the Asian female stereotype: "She's a strong woman, a dynamo . . . and she was mature, very intellectual." Nevertheless, each of the partners experienced racism from persons outside their relationship.

While the couple lived in the Philippines, Don was the victim of racial discrimination at work and eventually lost his job, and later when he and Patsy ran a small business he was often exploited by Patsy's relatives and acquaintances, who took him for an easy target. Patsy, who "had connections," managed to keep her marriage and family in "good standing" in the community despite disapproval by her extended family and others. When the couple moved to the United States, it was Patsy's turn to experience discrimination. When Patsy tried to be active in the church that the couple attended she became aware, as Don says, that "people don't recognize [her contributions] or they put her down . . . because she's Asian." In her interview, Patsy remarks several times that she finds some Americans to be "nasty and negative" and that she's had to learn to deal with "people tell[ing] you something that is totally outrageous, that's a projection of their own prejudices." She also has discovered that Don is perceived "as a criminal" by some simply because he happens to be a black man. Patsy despairs: "And what can he do about his black skin? Nothing! Until he dies, he will be a criminal to some white people here."

Although over time race became much less significant inside their marriage, it continues to be the main difference recognized by those outside Patsy and Don's relationship. The partners deal with incidents of racism by talking openly and frankly to each other about their treatment by others and by not letting themselves become upset by racist remarks. As Don points out, "Now . . . we kinda even laugh about it" and Patsy indicates that because "we have a good relationship . . . we are able together to deal with it [racism]."

This couple, like the others, has found effective ways of withstanding the racism of outsiders.

Judith (British) and Walton (African American), one of the couples whose narratives are included in this study, were also very much aware of their racial difference in the beginning. Judith, like Patsy with her spouse, recollects that before getting to know Walton she could not have imagined being married to a black man.

> Who would have thought that my destiny would turn up in the guise of some brown skinned, kinky haired, baggy-eyed, button-down collar, black American (Johnson and Johnson 1994, 193).

When Judith got to know Walton and realized that he was "wonderful ... noble and valiant, and stood head and shoulders above the rest of the other young men I had met" (193), race no longer mattered and the "racial component ... between the two of us [since then] did not exist" (195).

Walton, who had experienced a great deal of racism from Whites, was not attracted to Judith at first, seeing her skin color as a barrier.

> During my youth, I was subjected to institutionalized segregation and debilitating personal discrimination. . . . I do not feel I was particularly attracted to people of different races. In fact, given my previous experiences, I suspect Judith's being white was more of a negative factor for me (197–98).

However, as he got to know Judith, Walton fell in love with her and stopped focusing on their racial differences. "The different race was ignored. . . . Inside our marriage . . . we are not constantly conscious of being an interracial couple" (199–200).

Like George and Nancy, Adida and Steven, and Patsy and Don, Judith and Walton are quite aware of outsiders' attaching importance to the interracial aspect of their marriage. In their narratives, the partners discuss at length having to deal with the reactions of the respective racial groups into which they married, their families, and the communities in which they had lived. Judith especially recalls a number of hurtful situations and incidents to which she and her children were subjected.

[117]

> When I was first married there [were] some tensions between myself and black women my age. I was seen as an intruder who had absconded with a valued possession. I think [now] that the perception is valid since eligible professional black males are at a premium, and the response seems legitimate... (195). I have found that as a black man's mate... my husband would be greeted and fussed over by the [black] ladies, thereby acknowledging him as a sexual being, [while] I am forced into an asexual sterile role (196).

Judith also recalls an incident when her daughter, who was then two years old, was running ahead of her in a supermarket and an elderly white woman scooped the child up in her arms and began talking to her. When Judith approached she realized that the woman was saying, "I don't blame you darling, it's that !!!!!! [expletive] of a mother." Judith was extremely upset by this: "When I told Walton he was furious, but there was not much he had not experienced in American race relations... it was the first time that I... experienced malevolence, and I was completely unprepared" (196).

Over time, Judith learned not to let such incidents bother her and she became more confident about when to respond to them:

> I don't spend much time worrying about other people's response to our marriage, if you disapprove, that's your right and not my problem; however, if you impinge on my rights just a fraction and I have the means of redress, then I'll respond" (195).

Race significantly affected Judith and Walton's family (the couple and their three children) when deciding how to raise their son and daughters. As Walton explains, "We consciously encouraged our children to identify as black. In our view, this simply was the social reality in which they had to live" (200). And Judith adds: "They are perceived as black by society, so why prepare them to be any other?" (197). Judith also confesses that while the decision to bring up the couple's children as African American was not easy for her, she realized it was the right thing to do when her teenage daughters, at a time when adolescents explore their attraction to members of the opposite sex, were treated as "sexless black females" by their white classmates. This strengthened the young women's African American identification and since they already had a strong sense of themselves as black women, according to Judith, "that was a healthy response to an unhealthy situation" (197). In large part because Judith and Walton raised their children to be proud of their black racial and African American heritage, Walton's family came to appreciate Judith both for herself and as Walton's partner. And Judith's parents, who initially were apprehensive about her marriage to a black man, also have been respectful and supportive of her and her family.

Despite the prominence of race in this couple's life, both partners claim that they place much less emphasis on race in their relationship than do those outside of it. As Walton indicates in the excerpt at the beginning of this chapter, he sees the race difference between the partners as a minor characteristic of their relationship; however, for those outside their marriage it is "often the only attribute" they notice. Judith adds:

> In truth, I do not think that between the two of us it [race] exists.... The dynamics of keeping a relationship alive and vibrant doesn't really have anything to do ... with its being interracial (195).

This couple manages to deal effectively with negative responses from outsiders and does not let racial difference assume a divisive role in their marriage.

Several other interracial couples included in this study similarly report the lack of significance of race in their relationships. Carlie (African-American Christian) and Gary (American Jew of East European heritage) recognize class and gender differences as much more salient in their marriage than race. As the partners state jointly,

> Issues of race are obvious particularly to those on the outside, but they seem less central to what has gone on inside [the marriage].... On deciding who does what work around the house, choosing wallpaper, making career decisions or arguing out the inevitable misunderstandings of daily life ... [this] comes from sex roles and different economic backgrounds (Tartakov and Tartakov 1994, 150–51).

And Gary reiterates: "From the beginning, I was surprised by how unimportant race was to [our relationship] . . . it didn't seem to matter that much" (148). He explains that what has mattered more to the partners have been differences in how each grew up—he with more financial security than Carlie had—and gender differences. Nevertheless, this couple, too, found at one point in their marriage that they noticed racial differences more because the community to which they had moved was predominantly white and not accepting of interracial relationships.

> CARLIE: We feel that people who are unaccepting of our relationship are suspicious of our motives. A certain amount of disrespect is shown. . . . Our [racial] difference was not an issue for us until we were [confronted by] the . . . community (151–52).

The couple handled this situation by talking to each other about how they were made to feel, joining supportive groups of like-minded people, and staying in close contact with their extended families.

Sarah (Jewish American of European heritage) and Frank (non-white Egyptian-American Christian) likewise find race to be an unimportant aspect of their relationship, and are only made aware of the difference through public reaction.

> SARAH: After being with [Frank] all these years, I no longer notice or think about that he has darker coloring and I'm white. It doesn't really matter. . . . I may be reminded of the difference when sometimes people look at us when we're together in public, but most of the time it's not something that I'm even conscious of.

> FRANK: In our relationship, we are not always thinking about this [race]. It's not something that even comes up; we really don't notice. It's only . . . when we're in situations when . . . people notice that we become aware of the difference.

This couple, too, recounts incidents of racism to which they have been subjected. Fortunately, having friends and acquaintances from a variety of racial and ethnic groups with whom they spend most of their leisure time effectively distances them from the occasional negative public reactions.

Intersection of Race and Sexual Orientation

For interracial same-sex couples, attention paid by outsiders to racial differences is amplified by those others' negative perceptions of the partners' sexual orientation.

Penny (Irish American) and Mae (African American), both of whom were initially quite aware of the racial difference between them, claim that it has become insignificant to their relationship.

> PENNY: [After getting to know Mae] the race thing just simply didn't matter to me any more. I stopped noticing it.
>
> MAE: When you're in an interracial relationship you realize that we're all human beings under the skin and that race really doesn't matter, that we can love each other across these artificial boundaries we create.

Nevertheless, the partners acknowledge that both of their families have problems accepting their interracial relationship, a difficulty compounded by the fact that they are also a same-sex couple.

> PENNY: It's painful... still to talk about, even though it's gotten much better over the years. But at first, her family... they didn't know I was white when [Mae] took me to met them... [we] were surprised by the angry reaction we got. When her [family] saw us, they wouldn't even say hello to me and told [Mae] to get me the hell out of there.... But [Mae] was really calm about it... and said, "If [Penny] leaves, I go with her, and you won't see me again." So then her mother asked us to come in

Differences Across Relationships

> the house . . . and asked to talk to [Mae] in private. [Mae] told me later that the whole family sat down with her and had this long discussion about how they had been open minded about her sexual orientation, and if that wasn't bad enough, but now she was being a traitor to her race and . . . how they just couldn't accept that, too.

> MAE: [Penny's] father still hardly talks to me. . . . Her mother [at first] didn't even want to talk to me over the phone. . . . They dealt with [Penny's] being gay by denying that part of her identity, but once she took up with me, a woman from a different race, a black woman, they couldn't deny that she was in a mixed-race relationship. . . . And both [sexual orientation and race] were hard for them to deal with, but one on top of the other . . . just made it that much harder.

After some time, Mae's family has accepted Penny, and Penny's sister and mother have developed positive relationships with Mae. Although race is not an issue for the couple inside their partnership, external pressures related to race and sexual orientation continue to affect the couple's choices. For instance, Mae and Penny decided not to have children because, as Mae explains,

> We talked about it early on and agreed that we have enough to deal with as a lesbian interracial couple. If we adopted a kid or had a kid through artificial insemination that child would have to struggle with homophobia and racism and we didn't think it was fair to bring a child into this situation. It's not that we wouldn't make good parents or that we wouldn't want kids, but we're being realistic.

Penny concurs,

> It's such a great responsibility to raise a child, under the best of circumstances, and in our situation it would be pretty challenging. . . . We would be terrific raising a child together, but we realize how hard it'd be for a child we'd be raising to live and deal with the world.

Other interracial same-sex couples report similar effects of the intersection of race and sexuality. Lee (Chinese American), who has lived with Roy (African American/American Indian) for five years, was disowned by his father after he disclosed his intimate, long-term relationship with a man of another race.

> LEE: My father was very upset, he basically told me . . . that what I was doing was unnatural and that no son of his could be a homosexual, that I brought shame on the family. He was also upset that [Roy] is Black. I think the two things together, that not only was I gay but also in an interracial relationship, went against what he could accept. My mother, maybe if she could speak for herself, would have been more open. But she couldn't go against my father.

Roy likewise encounters resistance to his relationship with Lee from his mother.

> ROY: My mother hasn't dealt well with my being gay. When I told her, she begged me not to tell anybody else in the family. . . . She's afraid if people know I'm not only gay but [also] living with a Chinese man, they will reject me and her. [Lee] and I are not open about our relationship when family members are around because of my mother's wish. . . . I don't want to upset my mother . . . she's not in the best of health.

Despite the lack of acceptance from both of the partners' families because of race and sexuality, Lee and Roy simply do not view race as important inside their own relationship.

> ROY: [Lee] is just [Lee], my partner, and I could[n't] care less what race he is, what color . . . it [race] makes no difference to me.
>
> LEE: I stopped noticing that his skin color was different than mine pretty quickly. . . . Once I started to relate to him on a more intimate level, . . . as a partner in the full sense of that, . . . then

Differences Across Relationships

I stopped noticing that he is black—it just wasn't important. And that he is half American Indian wasn't really an issue ever.

The families and home communities of another interracial gay couple, Michael (British American, Jewish) and Joe (Cuban American, Catholic), reacted with hostility when they became open about their relationship.

MICHAEL: After we were together maybe a year or so, I took [Joe] back home to introduce him to my parents and the family and the neighbors I grew up with. People knew I was gay already and they were sort of lukewarm about it. But I figured, hey, this guy is the best thing that ever happened to me and I wanted to share my happiness with the people I loved and who cared about me. . . . Well, was I in for a shock! My family didn't exactly throw us out, but they made it really uncomfortable for us to be around. . . . Some of the neighbors wouldn't even talk to me, and other people even made racist and homophobic remarks. . . . I think it was [Joe's] dark skin that set them off, and that we are gay made it even harder for them to digest.

JOE: I couldn't really be out in the community I grew up in. I came out when I left [the community] and I was able to tell only my parents and my sister that I was gay, which did not make my parents very happy. When I told them about [Michael], you would have thought I [had] committed some kind of crime. They couldn't accept that not only was I living with a white guy, but [also] a Jewish one. Needless to say, my parents have not spoken to me since then and I have not been back home in four years.

Like the many couples already included in this chapter, Joe and Michael feel that race does not matter to them inside their relationship and that they find ways to deal with the racism and homophobia of outsiders. As with some of the other interracial partnerships, Joe and Michael have found a hospitable diverse community in which to live.

EFFECTIVE RESPONSES TO OUTSIDERS' RACISM

For the interracial couples in the study, race does not constitute an important difference in the sense that it is not a source of problems or conflict for the partners.³ Sometimes the reminders by outsiders are painful, as in the case of the black partner rejected by her white in-laws or the white mother whose brown-skinned daughter is perceived as not her biological child. For interracial same-sex partners, differences of race are augmented by sexual orientation, an intersection that sometimes sparks negative reactions by family members and others.

How do these partners not allow outsiders' racism—and homophobia—to significantly affect their own relationships? Mark Orbe and Tina Harris (2001), drawing on a model of interracial relationship development (Foeman and Nance 1999), argue that in order for interracial relationships to withstand external pressure, they need to progress through four stages that allow the partners to maintain a successful union. The first stage involves racial awareness or recognition that the other is from a different socially defined "racial" group and what that means for each of the partners. During this phase of the relationship, the partners address their awareness of race and develop mutual trust. For example, as the partner of color shares her experience of racism with her white counterpart, the white partner needs to demonstrate empathy and sensitivity to her account and point of view; in turn, the partner of color may need to remind herself that racism could be something new to and not personally experienced by her white partner. Coping with racism constitutes the second stage of the relationship development, in which "the couple develops skills to protect them[selves] from external forces (people, situations, contexts) that may harm them as individuals and as a couple" (Orbe and Harris 2001, 184). The couple partners thus determine which coping strategies are most effective to counter external pressures that could potentially break up their relationship. The third stage is identity development. Once the couple is able to successfully manage the preservation of the relationship, "Instead of accepting society's definition of what it means to be an interracial couple, the couple creates their own perspective and definition of the relationship" (ibid.). This effectively constitutes the forging of a relational identity in which partners incorporate each other's social group standpoints as well as personal views and perceptions into their self-conceptions (Gaines and Liu 2000). The last stage, related to coping, involves relationship maintenance wherein the partners periodically reexamine the role of race in their relationship and continue to develop ways to adjust to its effects.

As the accounts of the interracial couples in this study indicate, the partner relationships progressed through the above stages of development, albeit not in the linear sequence the model suggests.[4] All of the couples certainly were aware of their "race" differences and most report sharing and talking about experiences of racism. In some cases, as for instance that of Patsy (Filipina) and Don (African American), specific contexts created circumstances whereby partners became particularly sensitive to and understanding of the other's perspective. Thus, although Patsy was quite aware of the racism Don experienced in the Philippines, when she joined her husband in being an object of racism in the United States, she became much more empathetic to Don's plight. Given his personal experience, he could empathize with her, too. And, as we have seen, Carlie (African-American Christian) and Gary (American Jew of East European descent) became more aware of their racial difference and discussed it more frequently when the difference was noticed by others in a predominantly white community.

The interracial couples have developed a number of effective strategies for coping with the racism of outsiders. Finding comfort in talking with each other, surrounding themselves with persons who understand and are sympathetic to interracial unions, and living in diverse communities when possible are the most frequently cited ways of minimizing the effects of outsiders' hurtful comments and discriminatory treatment. Many of the partners also indicate that racist incidents taught them to be stronger, to stand up to people, and to not get upset every time someone makes an inappropriate remark or looks askance at them. Most acquire strength from inside the relationship, from knowing that their union is sound, based on love and commitment, and thus is worth defending.

As I indicate in chapter 2, those included in this study have developed identities both as individuals and as couples that draw on their own and their mates' cultural and racial heritages. White partners, in particular, often remark that they have acquired a deeper understanding and appreciation of their counterparts' experiences of what it is like to be a person of color in the United States (and sometimes in other countries).

These interracial couples also demonstrate an ongoing commitment to maintaining their relationships. The partners periodically reexamine race in their relationships; although over time race diminishes in importance to them, it nevertheless becomes salient at certain moments and needs to be addressed. Thus for instance, once Judith and Walton had children, they decided to raise them as African Americans, teaching them self–esteem and pride in the black race as well as in their cultural heritage. This decision was not an easy one for Judith, so she and Walton went back to it periodically as the children were growing up and navigating interpersonal relationships and racist institutions. On the other hand, Mae and Penny have decided not to have a child because they feel that in contemporary society the child of an interracial and same-sex couple would encounter problems.

The interracial couples' responses to the racism of family, friends, acquaintances, and others constitute effective strategies for addressing and diffusing outside pressures. Without such coping mechanisms it is not likely that the partners would have been able to preserve their unions.

Religion

Religion is one of the most divisive and salient features of intergroup partnerships (Berman 1968; Glaser 1997; Kaplan 2004; Mayer 1985; McCarthy 2007). Although the majority of the couples in my sample (70 percent) consist of partners from different religious backgrounds, religion, like race, is not recognized by the couples as an important factor affecting their relationships or as a source of conflict. However, it is often a difference of great concern to outsiders.

The majority of the interreligious couples in this study are Jews married to or living with Christians (33 percent), followed by Catholics and Protestants (25 percent), Buddhists and Christians (14 percent), and Christians with Muslims (11 percent). Only in two cases did one of the partners convert to the other's religion. In one case, a Christian woman converted to Judaism, doing so voluntarily without pressure from her partner or his family. In the second case, a Christian man changed his religion to Islam because his spouse's father would not accept a non-Muslim marrying his daughter.

Differences Across Relationships

In most cases, when asked about religious differences, both partners indicate that they do not attend regularly a place of worship or usually participate in religious rituals. The dominant pattern of this study among interreligious couples is one where both partners do not practice the religion in which they were raised. Seventy-five percent of the interreligious pairs in the sample are nonpracticing. A typical response is offered by Suzy (Japanese-American Buddhist) and Russell (Polish-American Catholic).

> SUZY: [Russell] was brought up Catholic and I'm Buddhist, but he doesn't go to church or anything and my Buddhism is more spiritual [than religious]. I don't go to a temple. I try to live my life according to Buddhist philosophy, like finding a middle road between indulgence and self-denial, being compassionate and tolerant, but I don't follow any ceremonies. Because [Russell] and I are not religious, that we come from different religious traditions is not a problem for us.

> RUSSELL: By the time we met, I didn't go to church any longer except on rare occasions. And [Suzy's] not religious either.

Similarly, Raj (Algerian Muslim) and Elizabeth (Czech-American Catholic) do not practice their respective religions.

> RAJ: I don't practice. I'm Muslim, but not a religious one. For me it's more of a cultural identity.

> ELIZABETH: My family [members] were raised strictly [as Catholics] in a fairly conservative organization, my parents having gone to parochial schools.... They were raised strictly, but I was not because my parents lived through the sixties and they kind of backed away when [I was] growing up.... I was exposed through my friends to different [religious] denominations. I used to attend [services] with my friends, ... so I was aware of [religious] diversity, ... and I didn't really practice Catholicism.

Selma (Mexican American) and Banu (Asian-Indian American) had stopped following religious practices by the time they met.

> SELMA: I was brought up Catholic, but I'm not practicing. I'm a feminist and I just can't accept the Catholic Church's dogmas, especially about women, birth control, and that women can't be priests. [Banu is a] Muslim, and she's still sort of religious, but it's more of a personal religion for her, she doesn't go to a [mosque] or anything.

> BANU: [Selma] gave up Catholicism when she left home and started living on her own. I used to go with my mother and sisters to a [mosque].... I stopped going... when I went to college and now I still consider myself a [Muslim] spiritually, but I dropped the more institutional aspects of the religion.

Linda (European-American Protestant), married to Kishan (East Asian Hindu), elaborates:

> [Kishan] was raised as a Hindu. He does not practice that religion. He will participate in some of the ceremonies when he goes to his family's home, but he does not practice it on his own. So religion is not a problem [for us].... [Kishan] removed himself from his religion, and I had done the same.... I had already done that in college [before she met her partner].

Kishan concurs that religion is not a source of problems for the couple because both he and Linda are nonpracticing.

> [Linda], like me, is not religious. She doesn't go to church.... If she were a very staunch churchgoer, that might have created trouble between us.... And she hasn't been very emphatic about Christianity or principles that she needs to impose on me.... [Religion] has not stood between us in any way.

Despite these couples' reported nonpractice of the religions in which they were raised, outside pressures (especially those from family) to conform to some extent to religious practices and rituals, however do

Differences Across Relationships

exist. For instance, Linda and Kishan had a Hindu wedding ceremony and attend a temple with Kishan's family whenever they visit India. Suzy participates with her family in some Buddhist rituals when she visits her parents, and Banu still occasionally attends a mosque with her mother and sisters. Raj and Elizabeth had a Muslim wedding (without rings) and occasionally attend an Islamic center that includes a mosque. Elizabeth finds that Raj expects her to conform to Muslim principles such as wearing modest dress when the couple visits his family in Algeria. For the nonpracticing couples that continue to maintain extended family relations, going along with some religious practices seems an acceptable compromise.

Among 20 percent of the couples, one partner is nonreligious and the other attends a place of worship and/or engages in other religious practices (e.g., prayer). One such couple, Eva (Honduran Catholic) and Casey (Anglo-American brought up Protestant), have this to say:

> EVA: I'm Catholic and [Casey] has no religion. He don't like religions.... I sometimes go to church myself and I go with my mother-in-law and father-in-law.... I don't go to the Catholic church because I don't know too many people. But I go to [an] other [Protestant] church, and I feel like I'm doing something.... It doesn't matter what church you go to, you look for God.

Eva also mentions that she prays to the saints.

> CASEY: My parents were and still are pretty regular church attenders,... but it didn't take with me.... I spent a year ... examining the scriptures and reading Greek and Roman and Mayan stuff ... exposing myself simultaneously to different systems of religious belief, and trying to decide ... which made the most sense to me. And I couldn't find any objective basis for choosing one of the religions over the other, so I became fairly agnostic.... [Eva] is Catholic but this hasn't been a problem because, to the extent that she practice[s] it, I don't find it intrusive.... She's gone to Mass or church a few times on her own or with friends,... but she's not real devout.

Differences Across Relationships

Nevertheless, Eva's family pressured her to raise her and Casey's son as a Catholic, although Casey did not want him to attend the Catholic Church or be baptized. Eva went along with her husband's wish but finds the constant remarks from her family members and others bothersome and trying. The interference from outsiders, however, does not affect this couple's relationship negatively.

> EVA: People [Hondurans] ask me, why you married with an American man who is not Catholic? They don't like that. And they say usually they [those who marry outside their faith] don't get along. I say, "We don't have no problem."

Joe (Cuban-American Catholic) and Michael (nonpracticing Jewish American of British heritage) have discovered a way to accommodate Joe's faith.

> JOE: Religion was always an important aspect of my life. . . . When [Michael] and I started to get serious we discussed this a lot and since he wasn't religious we figured we wouldn't have a conflict as long as he was willing to accept my need to attend church once in a while.

> MICHAEL: [Joe's] religion has not been a problem for us because he's not fanatical about it. I understand his wanting to attend church. He likes to go to Mass and takes Communion, but he's not going every Sunday or anything. Sometimes he goes to church just to sit quietly and reflect. I respect that. I'm not religious at all; my Jewish identity is more cultural and political, but I can understand people needing religion. As long as he's not imposing his faith on me, I'm OK with it.

This couple also encounter negative outside reaction to their religious difference—Joe's Catholic family does not accept Michael's Jewish affiliation.

James (Mexican American), who was brought up Catholic but rejected his religion, was able to effectively accommodate Leila's (East European American) desire to practice Judaism.

Differences Across Relationships

JAMES: When we met we were both spiritual but areligious. She was not practicing her Judaism and I sure as hell wasn't practicing my Catholicism.... And it reared its head when we had kids.... When [Leila] expressed a desire to join a temple, a congregation, I had no problems with it at all. I mean, I think the reason it worked is because I did not have an attachment whatsoever to Catholicism and I had such a positive impression of Jews and of Judaism.

LEILA: [James] had already rejected Catholicism when I met him—I couldn't have married him, actually, had he still been an active Catholic 'cause I think the differences between us would have been far too pronounced to think that we could raise children together in harmony. But he had rejected not only Catholicism but [also] organized religion.... And he had learned over time ... to respect Judaism philosophically and then just embraced it culturally.

Despite this couple's successful accommodation of their religious difference, they do report that sometimes outsiders wonder why James is willing to go along with his partner's religion, especially to have his children be brought up Jewish.

In a few cases, both partners continue to retain their respective religions but also achieve some compromises. Mark, an Anglo-American Jew, and Mechtilde, a German Protestant, both hold on to strong religious beliefs and at first tried to introduce one another to their respective places of worship before making mutual concessions.

MECHTILDE: I took [Mark] to my Lutheran church, but he didn't much care for it. Then he took me to [his] synagogue and I found it confusing, hard to understand, and boring. Most of the service was in Hebrew, and I wasn't used to seeing the men sitting in one section and the women in another. I couldn't understand what was being said and what was going on. He tried to explain things to me, but I didn't much care for it. . . . So we talked about it and decided that I would go to church and he to the synagogue once in a while and otherwise we would practice in private rather than sharing one religion or practicing both.

MARK: She has strong religious beliefs just as I do, but we both believe that we can practice them ourselves, without being inside a church or synagogue, that we can talk with God when we want, where we want.

Susan (Jewish American of East European heritage) and Samorn (Burmese Buddhist) have also made a decision to continue practicing their respective religions after they married. This was possible owing to Samorn's generous acceptance of other religious beliefs. As Susan explains,

> He is very open to any religion . . . [Buddhism] is not exclusive like . . . Western religions. . . . And [Samorn] is extremely Buddhist but he's so inclusive . . . I can do whatever I want [to practice her religion]. He's not threatened in any way. . . . In fact, it's just made me even more comfortable [about Judaism]. . . . At home we have representative pieces of both religions. We have a little Buddhist statue and on the door we have a mezuzah.

In both of the above cases, the partners have encountered some negative reaction from families and acquaintances regarding their choice to practice their respective religions. Samorn and Susan report initial very negative reactions from her parents. Mark and Mechtilde speak of family and others' disapproval.

Intersection of Religion and Culture

For many of the interreligious couples, religion holds more cultural significance than theological or institutional importance. A number of couples observe holidays associated with their respective religions, such as Christmas or Passover, or make use of some religious symbols and ceremonies. For instance, Shana (Jewish American of East European heritage) and Dirk (German-American Christian) have this to say.

SHANA: I definitely [celebrate] Seder [and] Passover, which . . . as a child I perceived . . . to be the most important holiday. . . . I fast on Yom Kippur [and] Rosh Hashanah. [But] I don't go to temple. . . . I identify with a sense of humanity that's very Jewish, . . . so these are the cultural things I take from Judaism. . . . We also do Christmas, with candles on the tree. [Dirk] sticks the candles on and there's a dish of candy that's [traditional]. . . . [Dirk] doesn't go to church but he likes to celebrate the holidays.

DIRK: Neither of us is really practicing. . . . She doesn't go to synagogue; I don't go to church. She decorates for Christmas. . . . She's the one who does the Christmas tree with a little help from me. . . . When [Shana's son] was younger, we also did Chanukah.

Sarah (Jewish American of European ancestry) and Frank (Egyptian-American Christian) perceive their religious heritages in clearly cultural terms.

SARAH: For me, being Jewish is an ethnic rather than a religious identity. My family didn't go to synagogue . . . we didn't keep kosher. I didn't go to a Hebrew school. We celebrated Jewish holidays like Passover and Rosh Hashanah as family gatherings rather than religious holidays. . . . And still I always felt Jewish. . . . I think this . . . came from growing up in a multi-generation Jewish family and having the values instilled in me.

FRANK: I came from a family that was Christian but only in a cultural way. We didn't attend church, but we observed the holidays, especially Christmas and Easter. It was more the food and the socializing with family that was emphasized on the holidays rather than the religious meaning. [Sarah] and I feel very comfortable celebrating these different occasions together with family and friends.

Jessica (European American, Protestant) and Tony (Chinese American, Buddhist), while not formally practicing their respective religions, incorporate symbols from both into their life together. Jessica states:

"We're not really practicing our religions in the traditional way, but we always have a tree at Christmas time and color eggs for Easter." And Tony adds: "My religion gives me a philosophical foundation for my life . . . it's not like going to church or being part of a congregation . . . but we have a small Buddha [statue] in the bedroom and occasionally burn incense."

It was quite common for the interreligious married couples in this study to bring cultural aspects of their respective religions into the wedding ceremony. For example, Susan and Samorn had a ceremony that included aspects of each of their religious backgrounds (Jewish and Buddhist). Susan recalls:

> We had an altar where we put a photo of my parents, Buddhist beads that were his father's, a Jewish bible. . . . We wore Burmese clothes and sat on the floor, but we had a canopy, a chuppah. We just put a big scarf over us. He broke a glass.

And Samorn adds:

> [During] the ceremony we ate fruit that I cook[ed] myself. . . . And we had a symbol of my parents . . . beads for my father, and I took a footprint of my mother, and beads for the Buddha, too. We put [these items] on the high altar and then we bow[ed].

Religion is frequently expressed in cultural terms within the couple relationships. Since family and friends are often part of these religiously based cultural practices, it appears that the practices are not a source of conflict between the couples and the outside world.

In general, a partner's religion, whether no longer being practiced, explicitly practiced as organized faith, or expressed culturally, is not perceived as a difference that matters significantly inside the couple relationship. In only one case did religion create a problem; when one of the partners embraced a new faith, the nonpracticing partner felt that his mate was getting too swept up in the new religion and feared that a breakup could happen if the novice started to spend more time away from the partner. Nevertheless, the nonpracticing partner was willing to wait it out and tried to be understanding and supportive. According to many of the partners, often those outside the couple relationship, especially family members, exert pressure on the couple to conform to religious practices and sometimes even reject altogether the interreligious relationship.

Summary and Conclusion

Contrary to popular perceptions, race and religion are not of primary importance to intergroup couples in this study. Inside the relationships, race becomes relegated to the background, to be noticed by the partners chiefly when made salient by outsiders. Similarly, religion holds little significance within the relationships except as it relates to broader cultural practices and traditions. Like race, religion is often made visible and relevant through the reactions and pressures of outsiders. This is not to say that race and religion play no role in these couples' intimate relations, but rather that these categories of difference are not sources of problems or conflict between the partners inside the couple.

The partners are certainly aware of these areas of conflict and strife, addressing them in their daily lives together. Many couples experience substantial interference from outsiders regarding race and religious differences, but are able to respond appropriately to such pressures. Because the majority of the couples find effective ways to deal with these problems, they can be considered successful partnerships.[5] In the following chapter, I examine more closely the strategies that the partners develop and use to resolve conflict and disagreement. By negotiating the differences that matter to them and to some extent those that matter to outsiders, most of the couples in this study are able to achieve accommodation and to live in relative harmony.

5

Accommodating Differences

> So quite often when there are differences, it's because she's seeing it from one viewpoint . . . and I'm seeing it from [another] . . . and then we kind of synergize those two thoughts together and realize . . . there's value in both.
> —Paul (European American man married to a Pakistani woman)

Although racial, ethnic, and national variations usually are important in the early stages of the partners' relationships, for most of the intergroup couples included in the study, such differences lessen in significance over time and have little influence on how partners relate to each other. Some differences, however, remain salient, requiring considerable negotiation and accommodation. Economic class differences and related cultural expectations in particular are a source of tension for more than half of the couples in this study. External pressures especially in regard to racial and religious differences can bear down on the partnerships. The majority of couples do not find cultural differences to cause significant conflict between the partners; some struggle, however, with what they perceive to be fundamental dissimilarities of cultural upbringing.

The following pages illuminate how intercultural couples attempt to resolve and manage problems stemming from those categories of social difference judged as troublesome. I focus on the *strategies* that the partners formulate to deal with conflict within the couple relationship. For the most part, the couples are successful in accommodating each other, as I have noted in passing in the previous chapters. They adjust to or reconcile the differences perceived to affect their relationships. Such accommodations no doubt account for the relative longevity of the partnerships (an average of twelve years for the sample). Only two of the thirty-eight couples who were included in the study separated since they were interviewed or wrote their accounts.

Accommodation and Relational Identity

Accommodation is considered an important process in all interpersonal relationships (Aron and Aron 1997; Berscheid and Regan 2005; Cushman and Cahn 1985; Hendrick and Hendrick 2000; Rusbult and Buunk 1993), especially in intercultural/interracial dyads (Durodoye and Coker 2008; Frame 2004; Gaines and Liu 2000). Because accommodative behavior promotes the long-term maintenance of personal relationships, it is particularly important for exogamous[1] couples who negotiate several dimensions of difference between the partners. When individuals are able to refrain from responding in kind to their partners' criticism or anger, and instead diffuse the situation, such adaptive behavior facilitates and maintains positive relationships (Gaines and Liu 2000, 98–99).

Successful accommodation can be linked to intergroup couples' relational identities, which, as we have seen, are "positioned somewhere between personal identity and group identity" (Gaines and Liu 2000, 107). When constructing a relational identity, the individual incorporates the relationship partner into her/his own self-conception and, in turn, is less likely to attribute the partner's anger or criticism to faults or shortcomings associated with the partner's group affiliation (Fiske and Taylor 1991; Orbe and Harris 2001). As I have indicated in chapter 2, most of the couples who took part in this study evince well-developed relational identities that allow them to function effectively within their partnerships and within each other's groups and cultures. It seems, therefore, that the development of a relational identity fosters accommodative behavior among the couples and makes them less vulnerable to breakup.

Accommodating Differences

Strategies for Addressing, Managing, and Resolving Conflict

In order to deal effectively with conflict, the parties involved need to first recognize that they have a problem and then seek ways to either manage the conflict, so that it does not escalate, or to resolve it, so that it becomes diffused and ceases to exist. The couples in this study rely on both conflict management and conflict resolution in the process of accommodating their differences.

MANAGING FINANCIAL CONFLICTS

As I discussed in chapter 3, a major area of disagreement and frustration for more than half of the couples are financial matters—material possessions, money management, and related issues—a conflict rooted in divergent socioeconomic class backgrounds. How do these couples deal with tensions generated by their economic differences?

Leila (East European American, Jewish) and James (Mexican American, nonpracticing Catholic), a couple introduced in chapter 3, are keenly aware of the very different socioeconomic circumstances in which they lived until their adult years; James is from an impoverished, lower-class background and Leila from an upper-middle-class family. The partners recognize that their class differences account for their divergent attitudes and expectations regarding material needs and money and that this is a major source of conflict in their marriage. Although disputes over finances and related issues continue to plague this couple, the partners have been able to make some adjustments to each other so that their disagreements do not seriously threaten their relationship. For instance, they agree that Leila will take care of the couple's finances, and they concur that they will not reach a satisfactory resolution on economic issues.

JAMES: [B]oth of us recognize[d] that there was a disruption. . . . And once we identified what the disruption was, then we further concluded that . . . this isn't really resolvable, . . . this was not something that we were gonna change. . . . And so rather than changing, we developed a[n] "agreeing to disagree" strategy. This is one area that we're never gonna agree . . . this is not a top priority for me, learning about managing finances [She's] much better equipped to do it, . . . so it became her responsibility. [W]e carved up the responsibilities in the household so that it would minimize [the conflict].

LEILA: I will say that [James] . . . communicates . . . better than most men. He's willing to talk anything out. . . . We've been able to confront a lot of things. . . . That is probably one of the reasons we're still married. . . . But when it comes to security and money we just have such different frames of reference [that] there's no way to agree. . . . I've tried to moderate my expectations. . . . [W]e talk about it, and that helps some, . . . and we don't fight about it as much any more.

By "agreeing to disagree," dividing up tasks so that the partner more interested in finances takes on that responsibility, talking about the issue, and even altering expectations, this couple reduces and mutes the conflict over financial matters but is still not able to resolve it to the partners' mutual satisfaction. However, Leila and James compensate for the lack of resolution to some extent by successfully diffusing discord in other areas (e.g., childrearing) and generally being able to solve most of their disagreements.

LEILA: We are very open with each other. . . . [H]e's helped me to confront things as they happen and not to suppress my anger, . . . so we communicate pretty well and deal with problems as they come up. . . . We are both very verbal and talk things out. . . . When our [children] were little we argued a lot about how to approach them. Somehow we fell into my being the nurturing parent and he being the disciplinarian. . . . I disagreed with him about using fear to control the kids and we talked a lot about this. And so he toned things down and I also realized that a little discipline was not a bad thing, especially with [their younger child].

JAMES: Usually, when we argue over something that's not related to money, we talk it out. . . . Now I understand your perspective and you understand mine, and now we'll both make some changes.

Accommodating Differences

Similarly, Tony (Chinese American from a wealthy family) and Jessica (European American of working-class background) realize that the main source of conflict between them is their divergent attitudes toward finances. The couple struggles to ease this tension but it persists; over time, however, the partners have succeeded in reducing its intensity.

JESSICA: We must have spent hundreds of hours ... since we got married talking about our differences [regarding finances], but we just can't change it. By now we both realize that how I feel about financial security and how he feels is not going to change. Several years ago we decided to set up three bank accounts, one for savings and two checking accounts—one for me and another one for him. That way he can spend what he wants and I don't have to see it all the time. ... I think this sort of helped us accept that we won't change, and once we did, it actually became easier to deal with. We don't argue as much about it anymore, but I still get a little annoyed when I see him bringing home something he bought that I think we don't need.

TONY: I don't get as upset or irritated any more by [Jessica's] money pinching. As long as I have some control over how I want to spend my money, I'm willing to accept her wish to save as much as possible. I'll admit that this is not a perfect solution, but it's helped to cut down on the arguments.

This couple, however, has been able to successfully negotiate differences and resolve disagreements in other areas of their lives. For instance, Jessica pays more attention than Tony does to decorating and keeping their home in order, yet the couple agrees to share equally almost all of the household tasks. Some initial tension between them over relations with their families of origin has been resolved by taking turns visiting their relatives and agreeing not to be critical of each other's parents and siblings.

Julia (born and raised in the Dominican Republic in an upper-class family) and Sid (American of eastern European heritage who grew up working class) focus in their interviews on the economic class difference between them and how this difference creates conflict in their relationship. Julia speaks at length about her need to spend money, in particular on "very nice clothing," especially before her retirement as a diplomat, and reveals that Sid "[didn't] like it" and that it caused "many arguments between us." Like Jessica and Tony, this couple also managed to contain the tension in their marriage by having separate bank accounts, so that Julia could spend "[her] own money."

Leslie (Anglo-American) and David (Israeli American), who feel very differently about finances and related matters due to their socioeconomic backgrounds (see discussion of class in chapter 3), have also discovered a way to manage the conflict. David has gradually resigned himself to Leslie's more materialistic values than his own, although he admits that "it hasn't worked out the way I would have hoped."

Leslie explains:

> Early on, we would either fight or not talk about things [related to disagreement about financial matters]. Now . . . we're much more calm. . . . We try to respect each other's point of view, and we talk. But we also know when we've sort of exhausted all avenues of persuasion and that there's no more that we can do. I know that I can't change his views [regarding material things] very much; he's come my way as much as he could, and I've changed as much as I could. It's like there's this invisible line that we can't cross, and we either have to live with that, or not be together. And we choose to be together and to live with that line.

This couple has also been able to resolve other disagreements that stem from different cultural upbringing, such as childrearing and family relations. As David discloses,

> If you took [their disagreements] this whole year and compared it to ten years ago, we're doing a lot better. When something bothers me or her, we usually tell each other about it pretty soon and we talk. . . . It usually works; we can usually come up with a compromise that we can both accept.

Another couple we have seen who disagree about spending habits and come from differing socioeconomic backgrounds is Ron (African American who grew up in poverty) and Greg (Irish American from a

Accommodating Differences

wealthy family). Although the two have not been able to resolve the conflict, they accept each other's attitudes and behavior in regard to financial matters.

> RON: We haven't really come to a solution regarding this. I can't change and he can't either when it comes to how we feel about money and material security. But we are better these days about accepting the reality of it and so it's not such a big problem for us as it once was.
>
> GREG: By being more tolerant, I think, of each other's [spending] habits, we get along pretty well and this doesn't affect everything in our relationship. We can live with it.

This couple, like the others, has found a way to resolve most other disagreements to their mutual satisfaction.

> RON: When we disagree about something, we try to talk about it. We know that getting angry won't work, so we try to talk calmly and to take enough time with it. Usually we come to a solution eventually.
>
> GREG: I understand that sometimes in a relationship, especially one that lasts a long time, there has to be room for each partner to explore things the other may not find appealing. I'm flexible in that way. . . . We talk about our feelings. He explains to me why he's doing what he's doing and I tell him about how I feel about it.

The couples with significantly different partner attitudes toward financial and material issues, although not able to reconcile the conflict, settle on ways to contain their disagreements so that the dispute does not corrode all facets of their relationships. By accepting the difference and treating it as a kind of uncrossed "invisible line," they are able to tolerate and live with attitudes and behaviors of the other that they do not particularly like or would prefer to change. The *management of conflict* strategies the

Accommodating Differences

couples develop—one partner taking responsibility for finances, establishing separate bank accounts, agreeing to disagree—keep the disagreement contained and under control so that it does not escalate to a level that undermines the relationship itself.

RESOLVING CONFLICTS OVER FAMILY

The majority of the couples (close to 80 percent) report at least some conflict in relations with family members and close friends. The disparate ways partners connect with their children, parents, siblings, and other kin are typically recognized as a cultural difference, a difference expressed most strongly among international couples but also among those U.S. couples in which the partners consider each other to come from two distinct ethnic groups.

For instance, as we have seen in chapter 1, Sheila (African American) and Gabriel (Ghanaian) have clashed in the ways they raise their children. The couple has struggled with this difference for much of their twenty-six-year marriage and over time the partners have made significant accommodations to each other. Sheila understood the cultural impetus behind her husband's standoffishness toward their daughters and took great pains to explain to them their father's perspective, even though she did not agree with it. Eventually, as the daughters became older, they were able to confront their father and let him know that they wanted him to be more engaged in their lives. With his wife's support, Gabriel started to reach out to his children.

> SHEILA: He now calls [the daughter who is in college] two, three times a week. He goes to see her on weekends. . . . He's going today just to give her her cough medicine and take her out to lunch. He's trying to reach out to her. . . . In [Ghanaian] culture he would have never done that. He would have written her off. . . . He has taken many steps forward in terms of going outside of his culture.

In their interviews, Sheila and Gabriel discuss the strategies they developed individually and as a couple that help them resolve disagreements, particularly those related to their children.

Accommodating Differences

GABRIEL: What we decided a long time ago is that if there's a problem, we shouldn't go to bed or to sleep without trying to resolve the problem. I think that has helped a lot.... What happens is that sometimes I just have to withdraw and sit down and take stock of myself and say, "Hey, this is not [Sheila'] fault. You can't take it out on her." When I behaved in a way that wasn't right, and she also reacted the same way, it had created a lot of friction. What she's always done is count down and sit me down and "let's talk about it." I did not find it difficult to say "I'm wrong. I'm sorry."

SHEILA: We've gotten better over the years.... [S]ometimes you're in a painful situation, you say, "let's not talk about it, it'll go away." And we've done that. It'll go away. But it doesn't. Three months later it'll resurface. So I've gotten better at addressing the painful [with him]. We try to work it out. I argue my point, he will argue his point, and then we usually come to some kind of agreement.

Another couple, Walid (Lebanese) and Debbie (Anglo-American), participated in very different relationships with their families of origin that initially created problems.

WALID: I think coming from an Eastern culture, there's more of a close ... link with the family than [what Debbie had experienced].... The culture clash comes [from] the relationship with her family. They seemed cool [to me]. When [Debbie] left [on a work-related extended assignment] they used to call me maybe once a month; if I didn't take initiative, they wouldn't take initiative.... They wouldn't inquire, "Hey, what do you need."

DEBBIE: In his culture, there's this attitude that family is important and valuable and viable and we really have to respect it and keep it together and do family things together, even if we hate each other.... [T]hey have this sense of loyalty and belonging to each other ... through thick and thin. ... In America people separate from their families [of origin], they go live across the country, maybe they see their parents or siblings once every year. ... That's what I was used to, so I found the family closeness sometimes too stifling.

In addition, this couple's relationship was affected by the pull Walid felt toward the patrilocal tradition of a wife joining a husband's family after marriage.

DEBBIE: A thing that came up between us was this whole different cultural attitude towards husbands and wives and their relationship to their family. ... In the Middle East, when a woman gets married, there's a sense that she is leaving and formally separating from her own family and going into a new [her husband's] family. ... But I don't feel that way. I feel like you get married and you both leave your families ... you have ties with them, ... but you set up a new situation. ... I could see at one point that [Walid] had ... absorbed some of the traditional ways of thinking.

While the couple was living temporarily in the Middle East, Debbie made a trip back to the United States to visit her family after her father had been hospitalized. Her father's hospitalization turned out to be a false alarm, and Walid was upset that she made the long trip unnecessarily at great expense. Debbie reports,

He said to me on the phone, "You have to decide between them and me. When you married me, you chose to be in my family, so I think you should just change your ticket and come home now."

Walid explains his behavior thus:

She got a call from her mom saying her dad went to the hospital, and then we find out afterwards that it was not a big deal. ... So that really pissed me off. ... [T]he anger came because of previous behavior by especially her mother that drove me crazy [referring to the cool treatment he received].

Accommodating Differences

Despite the seriousness of this incident, the couple was able to resolve the disagreement.

> DEBBIE: It was very clear that I'd have to talk to him about this. I was like, "Don't make me choose between them and you. . . . I told him, "I don't like this!" . . . it made me feel like a . . . piece of property that was moved from house A to house B, and I don't like to be thought of that way. I'm not ever gonna choose between him and my parents. I want both . . . and he settled down and hasn't raised that [particular issue] any more. It's no longer an issue, . . . we worked it out, and . . . now that's behind us.

> WALID: I don't hold things in, and sometimes I let my emotions out too much. I recognize that . . . I over react, . . . but I also rationalize my emotions, I use logic to understand why I did that [asked Debbie to choose between him and her family]. We talked a lot about it, communicated a lot. . . . That's how we worked it out.

Mae (African American from the South) and Penny (Irish American from the East Coast) experienced conflict over how each related to her family of origin. Mae grew up in a large, close family "where everybody knew your business and people advised me all the time how I should live my life." In contrast, Penny lived most of her life in a small nuclear family, without close relatives, and valued her privacy.

> MAE: [After] my family accepted her, they all started to talk to her about how she should run her life. Like, my aunt, my mother's sister, who I'm very close to, sat her down and told her she should go to graduate school and get her business degree, because otherwise she's not gonna get anywhere. And she kept calling afterwards to see if [Penny] did what she advised her to do. And my brother, [Ken], who lives near us, drops by all the time, takes stuff out of the fridge, . . . has the run of the place, like it's his own. To me, that's how family is and I don't get upset about it, but for [Penny] that took some getting used to and she still thinks I let my relatives intrude too much on us.

[147]

Accommodating Differences

PENNY: As soon as I met [Mae], I was struck by this almost blind allegiance she had to her family. . . . You couldn't even suggest that maybe her brother, who was over at her place all the time, was taking advantage of her generosity; she'd just be down at your throat even at the suggestion. They were just so tight. Me, I already had a lot of distance from my family and could see them more critically. . . . Every time [Ken] came over we'd have an argument about him taking advantage and sometimes, too, when her other relatives would butt in and try to tell me what to do.

Despite their very different attitudes regarding family relations, the partners have been able to overcome the problem.

PENNY: At first we yelled at each other, but then we realized that that's not gonna work, because . . . nothing got resolved that way. So slowly, we . . . started to talk more and were more calm, and we found that by explaining to each other how we felt, or why we felt a certain way, we could actually, well, over time, after a few discussions, we could come to some sort of . . . resolution.

MAE: [Penny's] not shy about letting me know how she feels! From the very beginning, she just told me straight out when my family was bugging her and I'd try to explain to her . . . where they were coming from, so she'd understand. . . . Once I explain, I account for my relatives' behavior, she can see that they mean no harm, that they only want to help. . . . We used to argue about my brother coming over all the time, but we don't any more. . . . We'd usually have an argument after he'd leave and finally we both just said, "Wait a minute, this is getting [to be] too much. We have to deal with this." We talked for a long time and [Penny] told me that she understood that [Ken] was family and that I was giving him access to everything I had because that's what family is to me, but that she was also living in our house and she didn't feel comfortable with [Ken] coming over when we weren't home, that this to her was a kind of invasion of privacy. So, from that, I started to see her side of it. And

> then she asked if it would be OK to ask [Ken] for the key, and I agreed. We both talked to him about it. He wasn't happy giving the key back, but we also told him that he'd be welcome over any time when we were home.... He still drops in from time to time, but we sort of set a boundary.

This couple thus was able to resolve a potentially serious conflict over family relations to both partners' satisfaction using strategies of mutual accommodation.

A very common source of conflict reported by the couples involves differences over notions of privacy and the extent to which family members and friends can be given access to the couples' homes and other resources. Andrew (American of East European descent) and Mady (born and raised in the Netherlands) disagreed frequently over the long visits from her family members.

> ANDREW: I've had to give up privacy when her family comes to visit... we have back-to-back visitors from Holland all summer,... starting in May until September or October.... First the parents come, and then the brothers and sisters come. The parents stay for five weeks,... and her brother for about five and a half to six [weeks], and her other brother and his wife and the two teenagers.... Her younger brother had come in the summer, and then he'd come again for three or four weeks at Christmas, and that got to be a bit much.... It was real tough... having people with us all the time... they'd be here in the summer and then you'd have a couple months' break, and another person'd be in your house again.... I basically had a big blowup with [the younger brother] at one point.... He liked to come and kind of take over... he would invite people over, and I didn't know that they were going to be there, and I'm cooking supper and there's people showing up, or they're spending the night, and I like to be... notified. I put an end to the two visits a year thing with him. I said he could just choose.... I caught a lot of grief from [Mady's] family over that, and from her.

Accommodating Differences

MADY: [Andrew] lost his dad and his grandparents, who raised him, probably six years into our relationship. [While they were alive] we didn't have a whole lot of contact with them, and that was, for him, also by choice. My family comes here every year, . . . and you get this "they're invading my home, my castle" from him. . . . It's really important for me [to keep close relationships with family members]. . . . It's not as important for him, but he knows it's important for me, so it's a thing that happens.

The partners report that although the long visits from Mady's relatives had been a source of conflict, Andrew over time has become close with Mady's parents and siblings and now doesn't mind as much having them in the couple's home. The couple has reached an understanding with Mady's family that they are welcome to visit them every year, but for a shorter period of time. Mady volunteers that she sometimes travels with her relatives following their, now shorter, visits, while Andrew takes that post-visit time for himself.

Emma (Pakistani) and Paul (American of European heritage) also experienced problems due to differences in how they relate to family members and friends.

EMMA: One of the things that most concerns me, and it's gotten better with time, is that I'm very family oriented. [Paul] is not. . . . It was hard for [him] to understand my $200 phone calls every month. . . . I cannot live without those weekly [calls]. . . . But [the problem is] not just family [but] also friends, just kind of dropping in on us or staying with us. . . . We've talked about these things and [Paul] certainly is a lot more insular [than she is] and very aware of private space. . . . I come from a culture where it doesn't matter if you don't have an extra bed as long as there's floor space. And whole families can stay with you for a month!

PAUL: In her culture, it is acceptable for people to just [say], "Hi, I'm here." Hey, it would have been nice if you'd called. No, they just show up. People will crash in on each other and just stay for extended periods of time; two weeks, three weeks, two months. In my culture, three-day fish smell.... And they won't tell you how long they're staying.... I want to know "What's your schedule, please?" for planning purposes.

This couple, like many others, has been able to resolve this difference by openly communicating and seeking ways to accommodate to each other.

EMMA: I definitely want communication.... [Paul] is more likely to sweep things under the rug, ... [but] nine times out of ten he comes around.... And we are both communicating ... neither one of us cares to allow a lot of time to go by before we resolve things.

PAUL: [People] are unique and different, ... so the differences—appreciate and respect them.... When you genuinely respect them, then you understand ... that they're coming from a different point or perspective.

Emma and Paul agreed over time that she would request her visiting relatives and friends to let the couple know in advance how long they would be staying and that she would try to limit the duration of their visits. Emma reports that Paul has become very fond of some of her relatives, especially her mother and sister, and "has been very welcoming of them when they have come to stay."

Celine (born and raised in France) and Bob (Anglo-American from the South), married for ten years, also speak of Celine's family members' visiting them often and sometimes even living with them for months at a time. Bob states,

After [Celine's] sister lived with us about a year, I was ready for her to move out.... And [Celine's] cousin lived with us for three months, and I was about ready for her to move out, and I don't think I want to have any more family members live with us mainly because my perception of what I expect from them is different maybe from what they expect from me.... It caused a little strain [between him and Celine].

For her part, Celine greatly values her family members' visiting and living with her and Bob, although she is quite aware of the stress this causes in their marriage. The partners, however, are used to talking about disagreements and do not let much time elapse before they address problems in their relationship. This couple, like Emma and Paul, and Andrew and Mady, eventually agreed to put limits on the length of the family visits.

Unlike financial disagreements, conflicts over relations with extended family are resolved by the majority of the couples. It is difficult to say why the couples are more successful in dealing with family conflicts than they are with economically based discord. When asked, couple partners account for this discrepancy by citing background economic influences on attitudes and behaviors and the problem of changing such deeply entrenched patterns. As mentioned in chapter 3, the general lack of consciousness in the United States of how class affects people's lives likely compounds the difficulty for the couples to deal with class-based issues more effectively.

GENDER DIFFERENCES IN COMMUNICATION

My study supports the now extensively researched communication differences based on gender (Arliss and Borisoff 2001; Dindia and Canary 2006; Dow and Wood 2006; Heyman et al. 2009; Stewart et al. 2003; Tannen 1996; 1990; Wood 1996, 2005). The research shows, among other findings, that women and men have different communication styles, whereby women address personal issues more directly than do men (Strong, DeVault, and Sayad 1998; Tannen 1990). In close personal relationships, as part of taking responsibility for "relational health," women are more likely than men to initiate discussions of the couple's problems and to insist that their partners engage in conversation (Rubin 1995; Wood 2005) and to facilitate the achievement of a mutually satisfactory resolution (Okin 1989; Ragsdale 1996). Gender communication, of course, varies by race, ethnicity, class, and other dimensions of difference (Orbe and Harris 2001), and this variation is reflected in the findings of my study.

Accommodating Differences

In the case of Sheila and Gabriel, the international couple mentioned above (and presented in chapter 1), it is Sheila who presses Gabriel to discuss their differences concerning the raising of their children and to communicate more directly and regularly about issues that the couple find problematic. Gabriel acknowledges that Sheila periodically sat him down and insisted they talk. Sheila reports that over time she has gotten "better at addressing the painful [issues]" and that Gabriel has become increasingly responsive to her requests for more meaningful communication.

Similarly, in Emma and Paul's relationship it is Emma who insists that the partners talk about issues as they arise.

> [Paul] is more likely to sweep things under the carpet than I am ... he will try to shrug things off if he can ... he's not the one to confront ... he still thinks that women would like to make something out of nothing if they can.... I'm trying to—I definitely want communication. And sooner or later [Paul] usually ... comes around.

Paul agrees that Emma typically initiates communication between them regarding issues about which they disagree, that she "helped me to see things from a different perspective," and that he eventually makes an effort to meet her half way. Similarly, Debbie is the one who started the serious discussion with Walid about not wanting to choose him and his family over her family of origin. She also made sure that the discussion continued until the partners came to a workable solution.

Sean (Irish American) and Elsa (Swiss-German American) also indicate that Sean "did not face up very well ... to situations of conflict [between them] where[as] Elsa tends to get it out in the open and get it solved." And Leslie (Anglo-American) and David (Israeli American) also admit in the course of their interviews that Leslie is the one who typically initiates "the hard discussions" and pushes David to "talk about the issues that are troubling to us like our different ideas about [material] things."

Most of the heterosexual couples in my sample acknowledge that the female partners begin and engage more readily and directly in discussions regarding conflicts between the partners. It also is apparent that male partners who are European American, white, and of middle- or upper-middle-class origins, are less open to direct communication with their female partners than are their minority male counterparts. Paul, for instance, was quite reluctant to recognize cultural differences between him and Emma, and it took a great deal of effort on Emma's part to engage him in meaningful discussion aimed at resolving their disagreements. Other couples with a majority group male partner speak of a similar pattern.

A number of previous studies have found that unlike heterosexual couples, lesbian partners tend to share responsibility for keeping relationships healthy because both partners tend to be sensitive to interpersonal dynamics and willing to work out conflicts to strengthen their unions (Blumstein and Schwartz 1983; Kirkpatrick 1989; Kurdek 2003; Wood 1993). Lesbian couples create the most expressive and nurturing "communication climate" of any type of couple (Wood 1993) and report being more satisfied with their relationships than gay or heterosexual partners (Eldridge and Gilbert 1990; Kurdek 2003; Kurdek and Schmidt 1987). All of the lesbian partners I interviewed—Penny and Mae, Selma and Banu, Stephanie and Claudia—indicate very open communication and readiness to discuss and resolve disagreements. These couples report having intensely close and highly verbal intimacy and well-developed strategies for resolving conflict. For example, Stephanie (European American of Scandinavian descent) and Claudia (Brazilian) share how they deal with disagreements.

STEPHANIE: We spent a lot of time talking this [a disagreement they had] through and she finally realized that this was something important to me and not worth fighting about.... It took several long discussions [regarding another disagreement] and we [finally] agreed ... we talk about it until we reach [a] compromise.

CLAUDIA: We put a lot of time and energy into finding a solution [to conflicts].... It's important to both of us not to stay mad ... we always talk a long time and deeply about things where we disagree.

Similarly, Selma (Mexican American) and Banu (Asian-Indian American) report devoting a great deal of time to discussing contentious issues in their relationship.

SELMA: We sit down and just talk about things. If it's something serious, especially if it has to do with our families, then we talk and spend a lot of time resolving the argument.

Banu explains that the partners "really pay attention to each other's perspectives" and when they disagree, they talk extensively about why each may have said or done the contentious thing, until "we both understand . . . where we're coming from."

Mae and Penny, whose communication strategies I examined above, also seek to understand each other's feelings and motives. As Penny admits, "by explaining to each other how we felt, or why we felt a certain way, we could actually, . . . after a few discussions, come to some sort of resolution." Mae, when discussing a conflict over her family's intrusions, acknowledges that Penny "just told me straight out when my family was bugging her." The partners then spent long hours discussing the issue, trying to understand "where we [each] were coming from," and eventually reached a compromise.

The lesbian couples in my study thus invest a considerable amount of time and energy into positive communication and effectively resolving problems that could potentially undermine their relationships.

The research on gay men's romantic relationships suggests that, like their heterosexual counterparts, they tend to engage in limited emotional and intimate dialogue and do not process their relationships constantly, as lesbian couples do (Kurdek 2003; Mackey, O'Brien, and Mackey 1997; Wood 1993). The gay male couples in my sample, however, claim emotional intimacy and report sometimes intense discussions and successful attempts to resolve disagreements. For instance, Lee (Chinese American) and Roy (African American/American Indian) state that when disagreements occur between them, the partners attempt to understand each other's point of view.

LEE: When we don't see eye to eye on something, we usually try to talk about the problem and to work it out. . . . I'd say that we usually come to some agreement. Like just recently, I wanted to buy this painting, . . . but [Roy] just didn't find it to his liking. . . . So we took a few days and then went to look at the painting again. . . . We went to a coffee shop and . . . talked calmly about [it]. He explained to me that he found it depressing because it reminded him of a bad time in his life and he didn't want to look at it every day hanging on a wall. That was enough for me. I understood right away that I couldn't get this painting . . . because it impacted negatively on my partner, and I wouldn't do anything to hurt [Roy], even slightly. . . . We try to be sensitive to each other's feelings and [to] how what we say or want to do impacts the other person.

ROY: [When we have disagreements] we usually talk it out. I give him my side of the argument and he gives me his, and then we sort of compromise so that no one feels like a loser.

Similarly, Greg (Irish American, Catholic) and Ron (African American, Buddhist) reveal in their interviews their strategies for effective communication.

GREG: We talk about our feelings. He explains to me why he's doing what he's doing and I tell him about how I feel about it.

RON: When we disagree about something, we try to talk about it. We know that getting angry won't work, so we try to talk calmly and to take enough time with it. Usually we find a solution eventually.

Michael (Anglo-American Jew) and Joe (Cuban American, Catholic) likewise pay attention to airing disagreements, making an effort to "understand how my partner feels and sees the issue," and attempting as much as possible "to get to that point where each of us feels OK about the situation and the problem no longer exists."

The gay male couples employ conflict management and resolution strategies similar to those utilized by the lesbian couples. Nevertheless, based on the amount of time and detail partners devoted to this topic in the interviews, it appears that the gay partners' level of intensity and engagement in communication is not as high as in the lesbian unions.

Moreover, the same-sex male partners report fewer disagreements in social difference (race, ethnicity, nationality, class, religion) than do the lesbian partners. Lee and Ron both claim that they "don't dwell on the different cultural aspects" and the examples of conflict they cite are more situationally and individually based than stemming from cultural differences. Ron and Greg, although acknowledging their disparate social class backgrounds and their unresolvable disputes about finances, do not report any other disagreements related to their social and cultural differences. Michael and Joe are emphatic about the positive aspects of their intercultural union and report no disagreements based in cultural differences.

A possible reason for the difference between the lesbian and gay male couples in culturally based conflicts is that the lesbian couples maintain (often strained) relations with families and communities of origin while all of the gay male partners are estranged from their nuclear and extended families and do not go back regularly to places where they grew up. Their social differences are thus not being reinforced by significant others. For instance, not having family members visiting their homes means that an entire area of potential cultural conflict is eliminated from the couples' shared lives.

In sum, among the heterosexual couples in majority of the cases, according to both partners it is women who initiate communication about the couple's problems originating in social differences and who actively seek extensive discussion until conflicts are either manageable or resolved. The strategies used by the female partners emphasize a direct approach to addressing a problematic issue, mutual listening, and "talking through" conflicts until an agreement can be reached. The men often address the problems more indirectly and are sometimes reluctant to engage in such conversations. Among the same-sex couples, the lesbian partners place more emphasis than do the gay men on managing and solving disagreements that are based on perceived social differences and report more intense engagement with the conflict resolution process. Nevertheless, my study reveals a higher than expected level of engagement in conflict resolution among the gay male couples.

Gender differences in communication also vary by race, ethnicity, nationality, and social class. Most notably, the majority group males

Accommodating Differences

(white, middle class, Anglo-Americans) in heterosexual relationships are least likely to acknowledge sociocultural differences between themselves and their partners and are reluctant to engage readily in serious discussions of conflicts resulting from such dissimilarities. Overall, however, the level of open and effective communication is high among these intercultural couples.

THE TIES THAT BIND

Why are these couples capable of managing or resolving issues that often potentially threaten the very core of their relationships? The answer seems to lie in a paradox facing intercultural unions. In a shared intimacy with someone from another social group, the points of daily commonality that inevitably pour into a relational identity seem to balance the broader perceived dissimilarities between the partners.

Most of the partners acknowledge that they entered the exogamous relationships fully expecting there would be serious issues for them to deal with due to their social group differences. Certainly, the couples recognize that many differences did exist and, in most cases, they disagreed at times due to perceptions of cultural dissimilarities. The partners are often surprised, however, that the differences are not as great as anticipated and that they discover many affinities between themselves and the "other." For instance, Linda (European-American Christian from the Midwest), reflecting on her very different upbringing from her Asian Hindu spouse, Kishan, who lived the first twenty years of his life in India, remarks,

> As I talk about this, it amazes me that we don't have more differences than we do.... It may be easier for people of different cultures to live together or to get along because you expect differences whereas people from the same culture assume [they are] going to have similar viewpoints. When [they] don't,... that can be a cause for a lot of conflict.

Although this couple struggles with differences in the partners' approaches to extended family relations and to childrearing, Linda and Kishan share a love of books, travel, and a deep appreciation for cultural diversity. As Kishan states: "We both enjoy being with people of various backgrounds. Moving from [the Midwest] to [a large northeastern city] has made us realize how much we like living in a multicultural environment, that it's important for our well-being."

Some couples discovered early in their relationships that, despite being from very different worlds, there are similarities between their cultures. Don (African American), married to Patsy, who had been born and lived in the Philippines until well into her thirties, recognized cultural parallels when he and Patsy were dating. Don says,

> it reminded me a lot of how Blacks used to court . . . in the [Philippines] she had to have a chaperone. And this thing of virtue—if you don't have the right intentions, then don't come around. . . . That's how it used to be in the South . . . you, know, getting involved with the family . . . and if you're not interested [in marrying my daughter] don't even bother . . . early on we kind of defined our values as far as [our different] cultures [were concerned]. I remember we talked about that [shared values] a lot.

Similarly, Selma (Mexican American) and Banu (Asian-Indian American) expected to deal with many cultural differences but, as Selma reflects,

> We actually found that we had a lot in common . . . culturally. . . . We both came from traditional types of families and neighborhoods with fathers heads of households, and mothers who did everything in the house, . . . where people had much the same ideas about how to raise children, and so on.

Sarah (U.S.-born Jew of European heritage) and Frank (U.S.-born Christian of Egyptian descent) also arrived at many cultural similarities despite their different backgrounds and religions. They discovered that their families and communities of origin share a kind of benign meddling "where people are in the habit of constantly scrutinizing others" and "where time was spent around the kitchen table talking about people, . . . examining . . . relationships and events. . . . People tell stories of the past and embellish them. . . . We both grew up with that."

Accommodating Differences

Celine (French Catholic) and Bob (Anglo-American Protestant) similarly uncovered important similarities between them.

> CELINE: We are not that different . . . we grew up in different countries, but . . . our backgrounds [are similar]. [M]y parents have a farm and his mother came from a farming family. . . . We are both from a close-knit family and pretty down to earth, simple. A lot of things I learned from my parents he learned from his parents, too.
>
> BOB: [We] have similar roots. . . . Her father's a farmer . . . and my mom grew up on a farm, the youngest of eight kids. . . . And my father's family were farmers.

The partners regard the farming family backgrounds they have in common as a basis for shared cultural values.

Other couples, rather than recognizing specific cultural commonalities, point to shared views and activities that are more important in their relationships than any apparent cultural differences. For example, Belinda (White, of European heritage, from a working-class family) and Luiz (poor Mestizo from El Salvador), despite very different cultural backgrounds, are united by their commitment to social justice.

> BELINDA: We share a lot of the same values, the same politics. . . . My husband and I share a sense of what community should be. We share a lot of the same vision about things and see the same kinds of things as being fair or unfair.
>
> LUIZ: We were involved in the same things [in the community] and we pretty much believed the same things.

Anita (Puerto Rican) and Burt (European American) have struggled with many cultural differences throughout their twenty-five-year marriage. However, in their interviews the partners emphasize the core values keeping them together.

ANITA: What is really primary is political activity in the sense of what are the ultimates and what are the right things in life to do. We both have a commitment to lead an ethical, moral life, and that transcends everything else.

BURT: We were discouraged from getting married in premarital counseling, but even then I, we, knew . . . that despite our cultural and other differences, we basically believed the same things about the really important stuff—what was basically just and what was wrong.

Similarly, Leila (Jewish American of East European heritage) and James (Mexican American, nonpracticing Catholic), despite profound cultural and economic differences, share underlying values and basic assumptions about the world that unite them. The family they have created together is extremely important to each partner (for James it is "the absolute bottom line," for Leila it is "the most important part of our lives") and they each are strongly committed to doing something of social value in the larger community (she promotes projects for not-for-profit agencies and he counsels HIV/AIDS patients).

Lee (Chinese American) and Roy (African American/American Indian) share hobbies and commitments to social issues. As Lee states,

> [We] don't dwell on the different cultural aspects; we focus more on things that unite us. We collect art, . . . we like to support local artists, . . . and we started to collect antiques recently. . . . HIV/AIDS prevention is something that we both feel passionate about. . . . We do volunteer work at a local AIDS clinic. And we're active in the Democratic Party.

Carlie (African-American Christian) and Gary (American Jew of East European descent) also participate together in certain activities that bring commonality to their marriage, such as traveling in Asia, being involved in progressive social groups, sharing friends and activities. Says Carlie: "Most important is that we share the same vision of how we think the world should be and our place in it" (Tartakov and Tartakov 1994, 151).

Walid (Lebanese) and Debbie (Anglo-American), whose different cultural approaches to relations with family members were discussed earlier in this chapter, express a mutually strong interest "in the Middle East and Eastern issues and politics." The majority of the couples in this study thus find that they have in common values and commitments that transcend social differences. Many of the partners acknowledge that these ties bind them to each other and help them manage or resolve internal disagreements and conflicts and also to withstand outside pressures that stem from belonging to different cultural groups.

Summary and Conclusion

This chapter has illuminated areas of conflict between the partners and how they deal with and attempt to resolve problems they understand to be related to categories of social difference. In general, the partners are successful in making accommodations to each other as they accept, adjust to, or resolve the differences they consider significant. Although this study supports previous findings that in intimate relationships women are more likely to initiate and facilitate conflict resolution than are men, the couples report overall a high level of open and effective communication. Finding similarities between the partners is a powerful antidote to conflict based in expected and/or perceived social differences. Recognizing cultural similarities and the shared values and commitments emerging from daily life together serves as a unifying force that seemingly offsets the potentially damaging effects of ongoing or unresolved conflicts.

The intergroup couples in this study exemplify how a homogeneous, essentialist "package picture" of cultures (Narayan 2000, 1084) is undone when people who initially perceive each other as belonging to very different social groups cross cultural boundaries and negotiate social differences on a daily basis. Cultures are not "neatly wrapped packages, sealed off from each other, possessing sharply defined edges and contours, and having distinctive contents that differ from those of other 'cultural packages'" (ibid.). This model casts cultural groups as separate and neatly distinct entities, thereby obscuring the reality that the people within these groups vary in terms of values, ways of life, and political and social commitments. As the personal accounts of these couples indicate, perceived cultural differences are not necessarily serious obstacles to developing and maintaining cross-cultural intimate relationships; in most cases their significance lessens over time. In the process of establishing intercultural partnerships, people discover cultural similarities and find that they have values and commitments in common that allow them to transcend their differences and form a close and lasting bond.

Among the commonalities are shared communication strategies for addressing and working through disagreements and conflicts that are steeped in the perception of cultural differences. Such strategies evolve over time as partners become more aware of what they have in common and as their cultural differences become less contentious. Investing a lot of time and energy into talking, mutual listening, and actively responding to each other's feelings, points of view, and requests lessens the negative impact of conflict and strengthens the couple bond.

Conclusion

Most people choose partners from within their own social groups and all known human societies have proscriptions as well as sanctions designed to keep members from pairing up with those who are constructed as outsiders or otherwise inappropriate potential mates (Goodwin and Cramer 2002). However, as ethnic, racial, religious, and national boundaries become weaker, more and more people establish intercultural partnerships (Lee and Bean 2004). In short, things change. What might have been unthinkable, or at least required the breaking of a major taboo for our grandparents or parents, can become possible, even mundane, with the passage of time. A black African woman marries a midwestern white American man; an African American man cohabits with a Mexican American woman; an Asian-Indian American woman marries a Latina Puerto Rican woman. Such pairings increasingly are not so unusual, yet, as with all relationships, there are challenges.

How do persons living in heterosexual and same-sex domestic partnerships in the United States cross boundaries of ethnicity, race, nationality, social class, and religion, creating spaces where difference can be negotiated and accommodated without loss or assimilation of identity? The thirty-eight couples included in this study have successful relationships because they effectively manage and resolve conflicts generated by their social differences. This is not to say that all or even most such couples form successful relationships. I did not include in the study intergroup partners whose relationships dissolved nor did I dwell on reasons why such relationships may be particularly difficult to maintain. Other scholars have focused on the odds against such unions (Bratter and King 2008;

Childs 2005; Curtis and Ellison 2002; Frame 2004; Gaines and Ickes 1997; Golebiowska 2007; Reiter and Gee 2008; Smith 1996; Zhang and Van Hook 2009). Rather, I sought to understand intact couples' subjective experiences in their partnerships and in relations with others. This, however, did not involve glossing over the couples' problems or the often quite disturbing and hurtful reactions of those outside their relationships. The findings that emerge from the study indicate that people are capable of forming close personal relationships with those whom they perceive to be of "other" social groups and that such relationships can greatly enrich the lives of the couple partners.

Individuals in intercultural couples are able to co-exist and live fulfilling lives in spite of sometimes quite threatening forces from outside their unions. It is not that they become "blind" or insensitive to their differences, but rather that they come to appreciate them, incorporate them into their self-identities, and perceive them as strengths while simultaneously often discovering similarities between their respective cultures as well as finding shared commitments and interests. Although some differences, like those stemming from class of origin, continue to be sources of conflict for many couples, most do find ways to accommodate such tensions.

Implications for Intergroup Accommodation

Intercultural domestic partnerships provide a rich source of data for bridging divisions between social groups in contemporary society. The United States is becoming increasingly multicultural at the same time that it continues to be riddled with intergroup conflict; it is thus crucial to understand how differences between various social groups can be negotiated and accommodated.

An intercultural partnership is not just a union between two individuals; it is also "an intimate link between two social groups" (Kalmijn 1998, 396). As partners develop relational identities, or ways of seeing themselves and of being simultaneously in two (or more) cultures, they demonstrate for themselves and others that divisions between "different" groups can be bridged successfully. Such unions also increase the possibility that partners whose origins are in hierarchically unequal groups can come to accept each other as social equals. In crossing group boundar-

Conclusion

ies, persons may relinquish negative attitudes toward the "other" as they become aware of the variety of individual behaviors and attitudes among group members. The outcome is especially significant in cases where the union of individuals from different backgrounds is not only tolerated by members of their respective groups but also involves the lessening of cultural stereotypes, prejudice, and ethnocentrism of the couple partners and their respective group members. An intimate relationship with a member of another culture "gives people an opportunity to realize the individual variety among members of another group, and . . . may ultimately weaken their prejudices and stereotypes" (ibid.). Such partnerships thus have the potential for contributing to cultural and structural change well beyond the two individuals.

Among the couples in this study, those who are accepted and supported by their families and groups of origin experience affirmation of their unions; their relationships in turn serve as examples to their respective families and groups of the possibility of crossing group boundaries.[1] Moreover, when couple partners maintain meaningful relations with people in each other's groups, a cross-boundary exchange occurs that can potentially lead to a breakdown of unitary and stereotypical views of the "other" culture. For instance, when partners' families visit, when the partners visit each other's family members and communities/countries, and on occasions when family and other members of both partners' groups interact, they have the opportunity to observe and participate in the lives of those in "another" or "different" group, learning first-hand cultural meanings and seeing people as individuals rather than only as members of a presumed unitary collective. Although the interaction of members of different groups does not always result in immediate mutual appreciation, it at least has the potential to do so over time.

Many of the intercultural couples in this study help create and maintain culturally and racially mixed residential communities. The majority of the couples lived, at least at one point in their shared history, in diverse neighborhoods or areas where they felt accepted and supported by others in like situations. The couples report that living and working in culturally diverse environments leads both to the appreciation and lessening of the significance of their social differences. In such settings, intercultural couples' differences cause fewer strains for the partners because the dissimilarities are not constantly called into question to remind them that they do not fit "the norm."

The intercultural couples included in this study are largely successful in managing and accommodating conflicts. My findings regarding accommodation strategies among intergroup couples bear implications for intercultural understanding and accommodation more generally. The study of achievement of cross-cultural understanding within domestic partnerships sheds light on how successful accommodation may occur between different (potentially hostile and unequal) groups. For instance, couple partners with divergent social class backgrounds and different attitudes regarding financial and material security usually are not able to resolve those particular conflicts. They find ways, however, to contain their disagreements so that the conflict does not affect all aspects of their relationship negatively. The domestic partners in such circumstances often accept their attitudinal and behavioral differences and treat them as a kind of "invisible line" that cannot be crossed and with which they agree to live. In other cultural difference matters, such as relations with family members, partners engage more in give-and-take approaches, tending to compromise, and generally come to mutually satisfactory agreements. Similarly, effective conflict resolution between groups may take place when each of the parties recognizes the boundaries between what is and is not negotiable, what each group can retain, and what each needs to relinquish in order to co-exist peacefully.

In previous work on coalition building across categories of social difference (Bystydzienski and Schacht 2001), my co-author and I indicate that successful alliances involve at the interpersonal level "a recognition and acknowledgement of individuals' experiential differences and identities that result from societal categorizations . . . an honest appraisal of how privilege based on gender, race, class, sexuality . . . is played out in the specific relationship . . . and find[ing] a common ground by accepting and honoring those perspectives, experiences, and insights that are shared between [disparate parties]" (9–10). Intercultural couples who took part in this study engage in creating alliances across social difference, providing living examples of how categories of difference can be negotiated in everyday life. Their accounts also provide insights to the development of structures—patterns of relation or practices—that emphasize

Conclusion

"respect and empathy [and] more egalitarian ways of 'getting along'" (11). The findings of this study thus contribute to a more general understanding of how differently identified individuals and groups can live together in relative harmony without having to give up aspects of themselves that they wish to retain.

Representation of Intercultural Couples in Popular Culture

Despite the growing number of intercultural couples in the United States, they continue to be an infrequent subject of attention not only among academic researchers but also in the mass media. As I have indicated throughout this book, relatively few studies have focused on such relationships. In film and television, the two most influential media in the United States and worldwide (Balnaves, Donald, and Shoesmith 2009), only occasionally have intercultural couples been portrayed. In those rare instances when this subject is taken up, the representations of the couples' lives have been deeply flawed. For instance, a recent television program titled "Modern Family" includes a married intercultural couple consisting of a white Anglo older man and a Columbian-born and raised young, attractive woman who brings a prepubescent son from her first marriage into the relationship. When the spotlight is on this couple, much of the storyline focuses on the lack of understanding (on the part of the Anglo husband and his adult children and their respective families) of the Columbian wife's and son's culture (reduced to facile stereotypes). All conflicts, however, end in the Columbian woman's acceptance, out of love, of the blunders and stereotyping. A reality television show titled "Keeping up with the Kardashians" is even more problematic in its portrayal of interracial relationships between two of the three white Kardashian sisters and their black boyfriends.[2] The black men are presented as highly volatile and unreliable partners who engage in frequent verbal altercations with their rich and demanding girlfriends. However, the racial and class differences between the couple partners are not addressed directly in these couple conflicts.

The rare representations of intercultural couples in film, even when attempting to address both the pitfalls and positive aspects of such relationships, also typically fall short of examining their complexity. When the now classic *Guess Who's Coming to Dinner* raised the unspeakable issue in 1967 of love and marriage between a white woman and a black man, the movie provided very little insight into the relationship of the interracial couple at the center of the controversy. Most of the meaningful conversations were between each of the (engaged) partners and the white woman's parents, rather than the couple—there were neither displays of affection nor scenes depicting difficult conversations between the couple partners themselves.

In the last two decades, still only a handful of films have focused on romantic relationships between people from disparate social groups. Here, I will discuss two films that start out promising, but that ultimately present only in a limited way the complex realities of intercultural couples.

In many respects an excellent film, *Mississippi Masala*, a 1992 Spike Lee production directed by Mira Nair, follows the development of a relationship between Mina, an Asian Indian young woman immigrant (originally from a well-to-do family), and Demetrius, a young black man of modest means who operates a carpet cleaning service. When the two meet, Mina is working in a motel that her father manages in Greenwood, Mississippi, where Mina's family eventually settled after being expelled by Idi Amin from their homeland in Uganda in the early 1970s. Demetrius cleans carpets in the motel. Their relationship develops in the context of the clash between their respective families and communities, which, while portrayed as interesting and diverse collections of individuals, are nevertheless uniformly opposed to this union. The couple partners, while exposed to the wrath of disapproving families, do not explore together the implications of racial and class differences they are facing; rather, the movie builds to a "love can conquer all" ending in which the young lovers leave the community so that they can continue their relationship without presumed interference elsewhere. One is left wondering what the future holds not only for the community Mina and Demetrius leave behind but also for a relationship that has not addressed the differences of class, race, and culture. As one analysis of the film concludes,

> *Mississippi Masala* remained unable to answer the questions raised by its own political work; even as it challenged long-standing histories of racism, the film could not envision a future in which cultural hybridity held a legitimate public space (Seshagiri 2003, 178–79).

Conclusion

A more recent example of a film that attempts to create a legitimate space for an interracial couple, but ultimately also falls short of effectively engaging the complex process of negotiation of social differences, is the 2006 movie *Something New*. Here, an African American woman, Kenya, an accountant from an upper-middle-class professional family, falls in love with a white landscape architect, Brian, who comes from an economically modest background. The movie contains frank dialogue about race: discussion of a "black tax" that requires Kenya to work harder than her white, mostly male, colleagues in order to dispel doubts about her competence; a black comedienne who makes comments about her preference for black men over white men; and Brian asking Kenya to take out her hair weave and wear her "own hair." The film also tries to acknowledge the partners' class difference: Brian does physical work as a landscaper—he is shown shoveling earth and his hands are often covered with dirt—while Kenya works inside an office or at home on her laptop, impeccably dressed in a suit; she hires him to landscape her yard and Kenya's brother calls Brian "hired help."

A significant scene in which the couple has an argument over race—Kenya complains that she is being treated unfairly in the office because of her race and Brian asks that she stop constantly thinking about race—leads to their break up. But, predictably, at the end of the film they reunite and are quickly married. There are no further discussions or negotiations of race or class; everyone in Kenya's family accepts the couple's relationship (ostensibly taking at face value Kenya's happiness) and ultimately they all manage to "get along." Missing from the film is a scene where the partners openly discuss how they will try to respect their differences and promise to talk through issues of race (and possibly class).

Thus even the rare film that attempts to defy stereotypes and to present intercultural couples in a less superficial light misses the mark by not fully acknowledging the categories of difference that are important to partners and omitting the mechanisms that partners develop to negotiate their differences.

The infrequent and limited portrayals of intercultural couples in the popular culture media not only help to reinforce stereotypical notions of these relationships but also suggest missed opportunities for more serious and realistic representations of these complex, multidimensional partnerships. The small number of television shows and films that depict intergroup unions also focus almost exclusively on heterosexual couples and thus contributes to marginalization by omission of same-sex intercultural relationships.

Offspring of Intercultural Unions

Intercultural domestic partnerships are contributing to social change as the children who are raised in intercultural and interracial unions form an increasing proportion of U.S. citizens (Lee and Bean 2004; National Public Radio 2009). Their growing presence already has had a significant effect on how we think about race and ethnicity in the United States, as exemplified by the revisions beginning in the 2000 census that allow respondents to identify as members of more than one "racial" group.[3] Almost seven million people checked off two or more "races" for themselves in the 2000 census (Rosenblum and Travis 2006, 10).[4] Moreover, bicultural/biracial and multicultural/multiracial experiences of children in intercultural families result both in the sense of being "other" and the recognition of strengths and advantages of belonging to multiple social groups (Coontz 2008; Fountas 2005; Root 1992). As the 2008 election of Barack Obama to the U.S. presidency at least partly attests, biracial, intercultural people may be able to use their multiple social heritages to appeal to a wide audience.

The offspring of intercultural unions find themselves in locations that resist easy categorization. They occupy "in between" spaces where new identities as well as "innovative sites of collaboration, and contestation" (Bhabha 1994, 2) are created that can potentially redefine group boundaries and societal norms. For example, a 2003 *New York Times* article about fashion and the mass media touted a new U.S. standard of beauty as the "ethnically ambiguous" (La Ferla 2003, 1). While the author recognizes the growing number of intercultural "marriages," and quotes K. Anthony Appiah's and Evelynn Hammonds' work on the social construction of race,[5] the article concludes simplistically that "many cultures and races are assimilating" (9). Similarly, a recent widely publicized book, *Blended Nation* (Tauber, Singh, and Goodman 2009), provides photographs and interviews of mixed-race individuals and families, but, as its title suggests, promotes a message of indiscriminate blending, reminiscent of the "melting pot" view of U.S. ethnic relations.[6] Fortunately, others have started to explore the subjective experiences of racially and ethnically mixed people and the various and complex ways they form and perform their identities (Fountas 2005; Hall 1996). Many Americans of mixed race and ethnicity challenge accepted prescriptions regarding intergroup relations (Fountas 2005; Root 1992; 2001) and help to build alliances between and among social groups (Barvosa-Carter 2001).

It is important to note that some scholars have continued to struggle with the question of whether intercultural couples and their offspring are helping to blur or blend social group boundaries or whether they are simply "crossing over" such lines rather than helping to obliterate or erase them (Lee and Bean 2004; Waters 2000). At issue is to what extent multiculturally identified people are retaining certain social group identification (that of race, ethnicity, and/or nationality) and whether some groups are at a disadvantage in the process. For instance, the higher rates of intermarriage and multiracial reporting of Asians and Latinos/as as compared to Blacks suggest that "racial" boundaries are not changing at the same pace for all groups and present the possibility of reification of a Black/non-Black divide.[7]

What this study shows is that the process of crossing into the world of the "other" is complex, involving both some blurring of boundaries and the conscious retention of essentialist identities, particularly among couples with partners from racial, ethnic, and religious minority groups (see chapter 2). To what extent offspring of intercultural unions identify with the heritage of one or both parents has been shown to depend at least in part on how such couples raise their children (Coontz 2008; Judd 1990).[8]

A recent opportunity to talk informally with the adult children of one of the couples interviewed for this study gave me some insight into this process of identification. I discussed the significance of racial, ethnic, and religious identity with Ana and Sylvia (pseudonyms)— the two daughters of Leila (Jewish, European American from a well-to-do family) and James (nonpracticing Catholic, Mexican American brought up in poverty). The young women were raised in the Jewish faith, attended a temple with their parents, had celebrated their Bat Mitzvahs,[9] and were active in temple activities for young people. As they were growing up, their father talked frequently of his poverty-stricken childhood and adolescence and they were occasionally exposed to their father's relatives, many of whom lived on the economic margins. While each of the young women has retained minority ethnic (Mexican American), racial (Latina), and religious (Jewish) identification from her parents, these dimensions of difference are not equally salient for Ana and Sylvia. Ana currently identifies more with her Jewish religious and cultural legacy than with her Latina heritage, while for Sylvia both her Jewish faith and Latina identity are highly important. Sylvia has travelled to South America, is fluent in Spanish, and has developed a commitment to social justice for Latino/as, as reflected in legal work she is currently doing with Latino/a immigrants. Both young women are in long-term relationships with partners who also are offspring of intercultural couples.

For these children of one intercultural couple, it is not simply the way they were raised by their parents that explains their social group identification; other factors also account for the difference in how Ana and Sylvia draw on various aspects of their social identities. Sylvia's darker skin and experiences with subtle racism is a powerful force that contributes, in part, to her greater acceptance of the Latina heritage she shares with Ana. A relationship in high school with a Peruvian boyfriend provided Sylvia with an opportunity to travel to Latin America; and moving to the West Coast after finishing law school facilitated her involvement with Latino/a immigrant rights. Thus both racialized experiences and situational factors played a role in Sylvia's stronger identification with her father's ethnic and racial background.

Which social identities become more salient for children of intercultural couples and how they understand and deploy their various identities when they are grown is still an understudied topic. This is a potentially rich area for exploration that can shed light on the debate over whether intercultural couples and multicultural and multiracial persons are creating an increasingly blended U.S. culture, reinforcing cultural and racial distinctions, or helping to establish new and more complex patterns of social identification and group relations. This book makes a contribution to the last perspective.

Those who occupy intercultural spaces straddle two or more worlds, potentially enabling them to recognize and counteract ethnocentrism, racism, and classism, and to appreciate and maintain diversity. As Michael Thornton (1992) aptly states, persons who reside in intercultural relationships

> carve out a new place in an old territory.... Each of these [couples and families] will fight a minirevolution, creating in themselves a new culture and a new society that value diversity and multicultural and multiracial influences. Out of dealing with these tensions, typically characteristic of those who are [considered] different, will come the creative social strains that result in a better society for us all (76).

Living in intercultural relationships is a daily challenge. The people who cross established territorial boundaries negotiate new identities, accommodate differences, respond to negative reactions from those outside their relationships, and link disparate social groups. Intercultural couple partners need to be recognized for their struggles as well as triumphs, their important contributions to the creation of a more just and humane world.

Methodological Appendix

A Feminist Approach to Interviewing

The practice of open-ended, semi-structured interviewing is a preferred method of feminist researchers (DeVault and Gross 2007). It allows the researcher both to identify topics and questions for study and to bring forth the voices and experiences of those she is interviewing, often members of heretofore neglected and silenced groups. The semi-structured interview allows for "an encounter" between the researcher and the interviewee, so that the interview is not simply a question and response event, but rather a more collaborative sharing of information and knowledge (Acker, Barry, and Esseveld 1983; Carpenter 2005; Reinharz 1992). This approach enhances rapport between the researcher and the interview participant and reduces the power differential that typically characterizes the relationship between the academic scholar and her informant (Carpenter 2005).

The interviews I conducted were more like conversations between two people learning about each other than standard interviews. Although I began each interview with questions about the participant's demographic characteristics (age, ethnicity, occupation, etc.), once I turned to substantive topics (e.g., initial meeting of the couple, courtship, reaction of family and friends, commitment ceremony, identity, etc.), I made it known that I was open to sharing my own experience of living in an intercultural partnership by occasionally interjecting a bit of information about myself. This often led to participants' questions about my views or experiences, which I answered honestly without providing a large amount of detail.

Appendix

The following is an excerpt from my interview with Anna (Russian woman married to a white Anglo-American man). She and I were born and raised in Eastern Europe and we both have been in long-term domestic partnerships with U.S.-born men. In this part of the interview, Anna and I were discussing the different ways that she and her partner, Robert, relate to members of their families of origin.

> ANNA: We [she and her sister] are very close and we also argue ... and I tell her things. [Robert] lived with his sisters for years and meets with them, but he always wonders about things but never asks [direct questions about their lives].... And he was never close to his father.... I was very close to my parents.... And I see that difference not just between the two of us but between my friends back home [in Russia] and here [in the U.S.]. Do you see that difference, too?
>
> JB: Yes, actually. I am much closer to my parents than [my partner] is to his parents. And some of my American-born friends are estranged from their families.

Participants were not only willing to explore similarities but also our differences. For example, in my interview with Joe, a black Cuban-American Christian man living with Michael, a white Jewish man of British heritage, we discussed the role of multiple dimensions of difference in our experiences with intergroup relationships. After acknowledging that we were both in unions with partners from different cultures and religions than our own, but that I, unlike him, was not part of an interracial and same-sex couple, the following exchange occurred:

> JOE: In our relationship, [Michael] and I have so many aspects of difference—race, culture, religion—and we're also gay, so that makes it complicated and more difficult, right?
>
> JB: Well, ... the interracial same-sex couples I've interviewed have had to deal with racism and homophobia directed at them.... My partner and I have no experience with such assaults on our relationship.

JOE: I think that it's harder when there are so many differences because in addition to the cultural baggage you have to deal with all of that combined prejudice from people who don't like those of us who step outside the pre-set lines.

Traditional social science research methods emphasize keeping the researcher's views and experience out of the research process. I am convinced however that letting the participants know that they and I shared the experience of being in an intercultural partnership, and my willingness to talk about it and answer their questions, encouraged them to be more open with me than would have been the case otherwise. This type of "strategic disclosure" (DeVault and Gross 2007) has been shown to aid collaborative interview encounters. Disclosing to participants similarities and acknowledging differences in social locations and perspectives can produce strong rapport (Edwards 1990).

The give-and-take of the interview as a conversation also allows the researcher and the interview participants to act in some instances as co-researchers. When researchers share with interviewees the concerns that drive their research, they may be able to engage in a process of meaning making and knowledge production (Paget 1983). An issue that came up in my interviews with a number of the couple partners had to do with how and why they were able to successfully challenge gender norms. This excerpt from an interview with Russell (Polish American man married to Suzy, Japanese American woman), who mentioned following traditional gender expectations in a previous relationship he had with a Polish American woman, illustrates the process of jointly making meaning out of the knowledge being generated by and about intercultural couples.

JD: Why do you think your marriage to [Suzy] is not traditional, that you are able to share household tasks and have an equal partnership?

RUSSELL: I think being in an intercultural marriage, it's like you're not quite in one culture or the other, so both [Suzy] and I have the freedom to take from our cultures, our backgrounds, those aspects that we want, and not to accept those things we don't [want] and to build something new.

JB: That's a really great insight. I'm making a note of it.

In this example, the interviewer and the interviewee together are engaging in the analysis of the "data," acting as co-researchers. Russell responds to my question with a thoughtful analysis, which later led me to ask a similar question of other participants and to develop an explanation for why intercultural relationships may tend to be more egalitarian than in-group domestic partnerships.

Ethical Concerns

The partners interviewed for this study sometimes reveal potentially painful details about themselves and their counterparts that they may not have raised with each other. For instance, a female respondent disclosed in her interview the fear she lived with, until her children were grown, that her husband (who came from a country where fathers had primary legal rights to children) might take the children from her if their marriage dissolved. She indicated that due to this fear she may have unwittingly kept her spouse from forming closer relationships with the children. Another female respondent said in her interview that she was disappointed with aspects of her marriage because she and her spouse had very different thresholds and expectations of material safety and comfort. Several male interviewees were very critical of their partners' close relations with their families of origin. And one of the male respondents mentioned that he had a hard time accepting a monogamous relationship and struggled with ambivalence about being faithful to his partner. A number of the respondents also revealed very painful rejections of themselves and their partners by their families of origin. In one case, a male interviewee disclosed that he had a very stormy confrontation with the parents of his partner but had not told his partner about the incident.

Although the couple partners are anonymous to the majority of readers of this book, they are not unknown to each other and their families and friends. How does a researcher working in the area of interpersonal relationships assure that very intimate and sometimes potentially hurtful aspects of such relationships are not learned by those she interviewed only after the research is published? How does the researcher obtain intimate details of the couples' lives without being exploitative?

As a seasoned feminist researcher, I have learned that the formal requirement of informed consent is not enough to avert the potentially damaging effects of information disclosed during intense personal interviews. Thus although I made it clear to all interview participants at the outset that I would not use their real names and that they could refrain from answering any of my questions, given the open and often free-flowing conversation during the course of the interview, respondents occasionally inadvertently disclosed feelings, attitudes, or actions that they may not have wanted their partners to know.

I dealt with such disclosures in two ways. Sometimes during an interview when a particularly painful revelation occurred, I would ask the participant if I could quote this part of the interview anonymously in the book. Other times, I did not become aware of the potentially damaging nature of a disclosure until after the interview had taken place and I read the transcript. In one such case, I called the participant and asked whether it would be possible for me to write about this specific part of the interview. In another case, not being able to reach the interviewee, I chose not to use the potentially hurtful disclosure.

In general, I have tried to avoid discussing potentially damaging details of the couple relationships unless I judged these to be particularly important for understanding the contexts and dynamics of intercultural relationships. Thus, a disclosure of infidelity by one participant struck me as idiosyncratic and not as significant as the frequently reported instances of painful negative assessments and even rejections of partners by family members of numerous intercultural (especially interracial and interreligious) couples. In the former case, reporting the disclosure would not have provided additional insight about intercultural couples specifically, while in the latter the frequency of the hurtful revelations suggests a pattern that could not be ignored.

Memory, Interpretation of Experience, and Truth

During an interview, as participants are asked to recall what happened in the past and how they felt or perceived events, they are actively interpreting their experiences even as they may be attempting to provide accurate and truthful accounts. The relationship between experiences, memory, and truth is problematic. The memory of experience is not equivalent to truth; indeed, "there might be multiple truths about an event without diminishing either the significance of memory or the importance of finding out what 'really' happened" (Al-Ali 2007, 3). Although there can never be an absolute "truth" and all human events have multiple narratives, we do not have to accept that "everything goes" (i.e., that all narratives are equal), especially when recounting stories of suffering (3–4).

Feminist researchers have struggled with the question of the extent to which experience itself can be considered "authentic" and thus could provide an "originary point of explanation" or "evidence" (Scott 1992, 24). While some scholars have considered especially women's experience as an essential ingredient of authentic knowledge (e.g., Code 1991; Collins 1990; Harding 1991; Smith 1990, 1987), others have been critical of treating experience as self-explanatory (Scott 1992; Haraway 1991), pointing out that it is "always mediated by cultural discourses and institutional arrangements" (Davis 2007, 132). More recently, several feminist scholars have rejected the "false dilemma" (Alcoff 2000, 45) of choosing between treating experience unreflectively as authentic or rejecting it as culturally contaminated (Davis 2007; Kruks 2001; Mediatore 2003; Moya 1997). As Kathy Davis (2007) aptly states, "subjective accounts of . . . experiences and how they affect everyday practices" need to be considered as "'situated knowledge'. . . linked to a critical interrogation of cultural discourses and . . . [social and political] contexts in which these accounts are invariably embedded" (133).

The process of remembering further complicates the understanding of experience. Remembering does not constitute the passive retrieval of information from a stored collection of memories; "[r]ather, the remembering actively creates the meaning of the past in the act of remembering" (Smith and Watson 2001, 16). The process of remembering experiences from the past is complex, allowing for reconstruction of one's lived encounters, encounters that were initially already shaped by the subject's location. Moreover, people's recollections of their pasts change over time as they add new experiences to previously acquired memories. The issue for the researcher/interviewer is how, in turn, to "interpret" what she is told by the interviewee. If indeed not "everything goes," then how does she separate accounts that are "credible" (read: truthful) from those that are not? Is making such a distinction possible?

Memory and the interpretation of experience play an important part in the construction of intercultural couples' shared lives, which is the subject of this book. Although not all of the couples I interviewed had been together a long time, all had been attached long enough (at least two years) to create "shared histories" in the sense of having gone through courtship, establishing a domicile and at least a semblance of a daily routine, and having developed relationships as a couple with persons outside their unions. I did not find that the individual partners' accounts differed significantly from each other within the couples, but I sometimes did struggle with the way some couples remembered and interpreted various encounters and events.

For instance, I was skeptical during interviews when interracial partners, after disclosing that they have been victims of racial prejudice and discrimination from family members and strangers, declared that race has not "mattered" to them inside the couple. I assumed that, surely, at various points in any interracial relationship external events of racism would have caused tension between the partners. After all, living in a racist society, how can an interracial couple avoid racial conflict? Were the couples being "color blind"? Were they presenting a harmonious image for the researcher? Did they conveniently "forget" incidents in their history together that did not fit this image?

Because the interviews were relatively open and reciprocal, I felt that I could be frank with the participants and free to raise such concerns with them. Thus, in a number of interviews with interracial couple partners in particular, I asked how it could be possible that "race didn't matter" when they had just told me a painful story of being rejected by their partners' families? In several interviews where I explicitly addressed this issue, respondents pointed out that it is not that they never discuss race with their partners or do not acknowledge to each other the pain from racist incidents. However, they insisted that racial differences (identified by the couples mainly as differences of skin color) are not a problem for them in the way they relate to each other. As Mae, a black woman who has lived eight years with her white partner, Penny, eloquently and simply states:

> I always know in some part of my mind that she is a different color from me, but when I look at her, when we talk with each other, when we do things together, color is not what stands out to me. What matters is more her tone of voice, how she touches me, what she's saying, stuff like that; I pay attention to those things . . . I guess I'm just used to seeing this white woman all the time, and I know her so well, so even when we talk about race, and sometimes that can be upsetting, I don't think, "she's of a different race, so she won't understand."

On the other hand, when the partners talk about relations with people who use the couple's racial difference to reject and hurt them, they are very clear that race "matters" in these relationships and that, indeed, it is the most salient difference in this context.

The responses I thus received to my probing questions helped to clarify what the interview participants meant and ultimately led me to present the findings of the study following the couples' interpretation of their reality rather than imposing my own framework or categorization. Hence, in this book, I deal separately with the couples' internal relationships and the dynamics of various forms of difference, and the relations between the partners with persons outside the couple. On the other hand, I also recognize that many of the couple partners essentialized their counterpart's cultural groups and resorted to stereotypes when discussing cultural differences between themselves and the "other." I attribute this to the shaping of their perceptions and experiences by the cultural and political contexts in which they have been located. My analysis thus takes into account the ways in which the partners both crossed cultural boundaries and simultaneously reinscribed them.

Another area of concern regarding memory and constructions of the past has to do with how the participants of the study remember the early stages of their couple relationships. When the partners were asked how they met and to reflect on what differences they noticed, if any, between themselves then, the responses would be affected inevitably by their current understandings and interpretations of these past events and experiences. Because the interviews took place years, and sometimes decades, after the couple partners met and experienced initial attraction, courtship, and formation of a partnership, I wondered how well they could recall what happened and whether I would receive rather distorted, perhaps idealized, versions of the past.

My concerns were alleviated, however, when some of the respondents began to talk candidly about their own racist or xenophobic feelings upon the initial meeting with their later-to-be partners, thus casting themselves in a rather unfavorable light. It became clear to me that the respondents were not making attempts to gloss over unpleasant details of their couple histories, and were willing to address issues that caused problems for them, such as differences in how partners approached finances or in their childrearing philosophies and practices. I was thus satisfied that the respondents were making a genuine effort to be open and truthful about their shared pasts and their present relationships.

I am not suggesting, however, that the stories told to me would have been the same if they had been shared with the couples' friends, children, extended families, acquaintances, or with another interviewer, or at another time. We all provide somewhat differing accounts of events and experiences to different audiences and our versions of the past change over time (Smith and Watson 2001). Nevertheless, I am quite certain that those I interviewed, acting within the above-mentioned constraints, did not intentionally misrepresent their stories.

LIST OF STUDY PARTICIPANTS

Couple Partners	Years Together	Class of Origin	Race	Ethnicity/ Nationality	Age	Religion	Occupation
Sheila & Gabriel	26	Lower/ Upper	Black/ Black	African American/ Ghanaian	50/51	Baptist/ Methodist	HR director/ VP operations
Suzy & Russell	7	Middle/ Lower Middle	Asian/ White	Japanese American/ Polish American	29/31	Buddhist/ Catholic	Dental hygienist/ Self-employed business owner
Selma & Banu	3	Lower/ Middle	Latina/ Asian	Mexican American/ Asian-Indian American	26/28	Catholic (nonprac.)/ Muslim	Community organizer/ Computer programmer
Patsy & Don	14	Middle/ Working	Asian/ Black	Filipina/ African American	46/49	Baptist/ Baptist	Restaurant server/ Counselor
Belinda & Luiz	12	Working/ Lower	White/ Latino	European American/ Salvadoran	37/31	Protestant/ Catholic	Social worker/ Maintenance mechanic
Jerry & Hege	36	Working/ Upper Middle	White/ White	Anglo-American/ Norwegian	56/70	Lutheran/ Methodist	Dir. computer center/ High school teacher
Casey & Eva	10	Working/ Lower	White/ Latina	Anglo-American/ Honduran	45/31	Atheist/ Catholic	ESL instructor/ Homemaker
Christy & Ayoub*	10	Upper middle/ Lower	White/ Non-White Middle Eastern	Northern European American/ Iranian	45/38	Catholic/ Muslim	College professor/ Engineer
Samorn & Susan	2	Working/ Middle	Asian/ White	Burmese/ East European American	47/54	Buddhist/ Jewish	Airport security attendant/ ESL teacher
Claudia & Stephanie	10	Working/ Middle	Latina/ White	Brazilian/ Scandinavian American	37/46	Catholic/ Lutheran	Marketing director/ Middle school teacher
Jessica & Tony	15	Working/ Upper	White/ Asian	European American/ Chinese American	45/47	Protestant/ Buddhist	Self-emploss consultant/ Landscape designer
George & Nancy	6	Lower/ Middle	Black/ White	Tanzanian/ Italian American	34/32	Protestant/ Catholic	Technology consultant/ Hospital administrator
Mae & Penny	8	Working/ Working	Black/ White	African American/ Irish American	37/35	Baptist/ Catholic	Social worker/ Book store manager

[186]

Couple Partners	Years Together	Class of Origin	Race	Ethnicity/ Nationality	Age	Religion	Occupation
Leslie & David	16	Upper/ Working	White/ White	Anglo-American/ Israeli American	43/50	Protestant (conv. to Judaism)/Jewish	Middle school teacher/ Newspaper reporter
Michael & Joe	10	Middle/ Working	White/ Black-Latino	British American/ Cuban American	33/35	Jewish/ Catholic	Librarian/ Construction worker
Elizabeth & Raj	6	Middle/ Working	White/ Non-White North African Arab	Czech American/ Algerian	29/37	Catholic/ Muslim	Graduate student/ College professor
Anna & Robert	15	Middle/ Middle	White/ White	Russian/ Anglo-American	41/50	Russian Orthodox/ Protestant	Office manager/ Freelance writer
Anita & Burt	25	Lower/ Middle	Latina/ White	Puerto Rican/ European American	47/51	Baptist/ Methodist	Accountant/ Minister
Sarah & Frank	12	Middle/ Working	White/ Non-White Middle Eastern	East European American/ Egyptian American	43/45	Jewish/ Christian	Midlevel manager/ Architect
Carlie & Gary*	21	Working/ Middle	Black/ White	African American/ East European American	52/51	Baptist/ Jewish	College professor/ College professor
Lee & Roy	7	Working/ Lower	Asian/ Black	Chinese American/ African American–American Indian	32/34	Buddhist/ Baptist	Statistician/ Business manager
Emma & Paul	6	Upper/ Middle	Asian/ White	Pakistani/ European American	33/46	Muslim/ Christian (conv. to Islam)	Graduate student/ Self-employed financial advisor
Shana & Dirk	14	Middle/ Working	White/ White	East European American/ German American	50/54	Jewish/ Catholic (nonprac.)	Homemaker/ High school teacher
Isabela & Graham	15	Middle/ Working	Latina/ White	Chilean/ Irish American	33/37	Catholic/ Catholic	Business publicist/ Carpenter
Ron & Greg	12	Lower/ Upper Middle	Black/ White	African America/ Irish American	47/39	Buddhist/ Catholic (nonprac.)	Accountant/ Graphic Designer

Couple Partners	Years Together	Class of Origin	Race	Ethnicity/Nationality	Age	Religion	Occupation
James & Leila	22	Lower/Middle	Latino/White	Mexican American/East European American	48/47	Catholic (nonprac.)/Jewish	Social worker/Marketing director
Amy & John	26	Working/Middle	White/White	Swiss/European American	52/60	Jewish/Christian	Homemaker/Business owner
Adida & Steven	4	Lower/Middle	Black/White	South African/German American	33/34	Catholic/Protestant	Graduate student/University professor
Judith & Walton*	31	Middle/Working	White/Black	British/African American	57/58	Methodist/Baptist	Homemaker/College professor
Mark & Mechtilde	17	Middle/Working	White/White	Anglo-American/German	52/46	Jewish/Protestant	Accountant/Homemaker
Debbie & Walid	3	Middle/Working	White/Non-White Middle Eastern	Anglo-American/Lebanese	36/42	Catholic (nonprac.)/Muslim	Organizational consultant/Journalist
Linda & Kishan	4	Middle/Middle	White/Asian	European American/East Asian Indian	27/37	Protestant (nonprac.)/Hindu	Homemaker/Business executive
Julia & Sid	34	Upper/Working	Latina/White	Dominican/East European American	78/80	Catholic/Protestant	Retired diplomat/Retired navy officer
Myra & Peter	32	Working/Lower	White/White	French Canadian/Hungarian American	59/65	Catholic/Catholic	Clerk/Retired clerk
Silvia & Bill	23	Middle/Lower	Latina/White	Peruvian/English Canadian	49/62	Catholic/Catholic	Nurse/Developmentaid worker
Sean & Elsa	25	Working/Middle	White/White	Irish American/Swiss-German American	59/52	Catholic (nonprac.)/Methodist	Airline supervisor/Homemaker
Mady & Andrew	15	Middle/Working	White/White	Dutch/East European American	46/46	Protestant (nonprac.)/Catholic (nonprac.)	Medical receptionist/Self-employed carpenter
Celine & Bob	10	Middle/Middle	White/White	French/Anglo-American	34/37	Catholic/Protestant	Homemaker/Small business owner

*These couples' self-narratives rather than interviews provided data for the study.

Notes

INTRODUCTION

1. It is important to note that the term "intercultural" has been used previously by others who have studied people married to or cohabiting with those of other races, ethnicities, or religions (e.g., Biever, Bobele, and North 1998; Collier 2003; Crohn 1998; Gaines and Agnew 2003; Reiter and Gee 2008).

2. The meaning of gender varies according to the context in which it is used, and in academic discussions there are several ways of conceptualizing gender: as a social construction (Chancer and Watkins 2006), a system of inequality (Lorber 2005), performance (Butler 1993; 1998), or values and norms that underlie structures (Acker 2006).

3. There has been a longstanding debate in the social sciences about whether class is structurally determined or whether it also generates "values and practices" that help to perpetuate the class system; for example, staying in poverty (see, e.g., Alexander and Seidman 1990; Crompton 1998; Skegg 2004). More important, many scholars, beginning with Max Weber, have acknowledged the role of culture in shaping people's perceptions of class (Bourdieu 1984; Chancer and Watkins 2006, chapter 4; hooks 2000).

4. An important exception is the study by Blumstein and Schwartz, *American Couples* (1983), which included married and cohabiting heterosexual and homosexual couples.

5. The inclusion of same-sex couples in the study also normalizes homosexual relationships. According to Seidman (2002), "The hetero/homosexual division came to serve as an important regulatory force ... as gays are viewed as normal, designation as the good or bad sexual citizen is less dependent on sexual identity" (160).

6. The treatment of experience can be problematic if it is approached unreflectively as an authentic source of knowledge or truth. I discuss this issue in the methodological appendix to this book.

7. I began the study with Estelle Resnik, who left the project after completing seventeen interviews, and I continued then to obtain more interviews on my own. Dr. Resnik gave me permission to use the interviews she conducted.

8. For twenty-eight of the seventy-eight individuals included in the study (or 35 percent) English was not their native language

9. In four cases, the couples communicated in both English and another language.

10. Nineteen of the thirty-eight couples had children either living at home or grown.

11. See, for example, Browne 2005; Bystydzienski 1995; Carlson et al. 1994; Childs 2005; Rosenblatt, Karis, and Powell 1995; Rubin 1995.

12. A representative sample is one that is probability-based and allows the researcher to generalize the findings obtained from the study participants to a larger defined population from which the participants were selected.

13. For their books on interracial couples, Paul Rosenblatt, Teri Karis, and Richard Powell (1995) interviewed twenty-one couples; Robert McNamara, Maria Tempenis, and Beth Walton (1999) interviewed twenty-eight couples; and Erica Chito Childs (2005) interviewed fifteen couples. Nancy Diggs (2001) spoke with thirty women for her book on U.S. women who married Japanese men. In her study of first sexual experiences, Laura Carpenter (2005) interviewed sixty-one young adults. Jacquelyn Litt interviewed thirty-eight women for her book *Medicalized Motherhood* (2000).

14. In two cases the interviews were conducted by telephone, as respondents were not available in person.

15. We followed the referrals across these states. In some cases, this was facilitated by job related changes in our respective places of residence.

16. Since the additional three couples' narratives had been published, I used their real names and did not alter any aspects of their backgrounds.

17. I analyzed the three couple narratives in the same way as the interview transcripts.

CHAPTER 1

1. This is consistent with previous findings that most people pair up with someone of similar educational and occupational status (see, e.g., Kornblum and Smith 1996).

2. This issue is also addressed in the three couples' narratives.

CHAPTER 2

1. Couples in which one partner was from the U.S. dominant group and the other from a non-Western country or domestic minority group constituted 50 percent of the sample, or nineteen of the thirty-eight couples.

2. Ten of the nineteen couples had a male dominant group partner.

3. For a discussion of how white privilege affects personal relationships of even consciously aware white antiracists, see O'Brien 2003.

CHAPTER 3

1. For a discussion of class beyond the conventional economic indicators, see hooks 2000, and Reay 2004.
2. Family sociologists and other social scientists have long called attention to money as a major source of conflict in couple relationships (see, among others, Blumstein and Schwartz 1983; Coontz 2008; Fincham 2003; Millman 1991; Sillars, Roberts, and Dun 2000). However, in previous studies, conflicts over money have not been linked explicitly to class differences between the couple partners.

CHAPTER 4

1. The reactions of those outside the couples were reported by the intergroup partners in their interviews and narratives and thus constitute their perceptions of their partnerships by outsiders.
2. With the rise in non-European immigration, the rates of interracial marriage have increased substantially. However, most of the increase is accounted for by intermarriage between Asians and Whites and Latinos and Whites; intermarriage rates for Blacks continue to be low. The 2000 census data show that about 30 percent of married native-born Asians and Latinos had a spouse of a different racial background, mostly White. By contrast, only one-tenth of Blacks married someone of a different racial background (Lee and Bean 2004).
3. Erica Chito Childs (2005) similarly found in her study of seventeen interracial couples that "All of the couples have come together despite any opposition that may exist, thereby minimizing the importance of race or racial boundaries. Within their intimate and everyday lives, the couples all stated that their race, or more specifically their racial differences, were not an issue or source of problems between each other. It was only when others outside the relationship highlighted or emphasized race that it became an issue" (41).
4. Foeman and Nance (1999) indicate that the stages can be revisited by the interracial partners and will vary from couple to couple.
5. By "successful" I mean that not only did the partners stay together, but, more important, they also expressed a high degree of satisfaction with the relationship.

CHAPTER 5

1. Exogamy refers to the principle of choosing a partner from outside of one's primary group, particularly outside one's family's social heritage.

CONCLUSION

1. The majority of the couples (twenty-six of thirty-eight) reported having the support and understanding of their parents, siblings, and/or other family members, friends, and acquaintances from their respective groups of origin.

2. In the last season of the show (2009–2010), one of the interracial couples breaks up and the other gets married.

3. The way "race" is conceptualized in the 2000 census is highly problematic. The census includes as part of the "race" question ethnic categories such as Asian Indian, Chinese, Filipino, etc., and provides a separate question for Spanish/Hispanic/Latino and national subcategories (Mexican, Puerto Rican, Cuban, and "other").

4. Between 2000 and 2008 people who identify as multiracial have increased by 25 percent (National Public Radio 2009). It is predicted that by the year 2050, one in five Americans could claim a multiracial background (Lee and Bean 2004).

5. Both of these scholars have written extensively about race; see, for e.g., Appiah (1996; 2005), Hammonds (2005), and Hammonds et al. (2005).

6. The metaphor of "the melting pot" has been used in the United States since the term was coined in Israel Zangwill's 1908 play *The Melting Pot*, to describe the fusion of different nationalities and ethnicities. In the 1960s Nathan Glazer and Daniel P. Moynihan challenged this view in their now classic *Beyond the Melting Pot: The Negroes, Puerto Ricans, Jews, Italians, and Irish of New York City* (1963), in which they argued that the various groups kept their distinct identities in a hierarchical system of ethnicities.

7. Intermarriage rates for Asians and Latinos are three times as high as for Blacks. The different rates of intermarriage among nonwhite racial groups indicate that racial boundaries are more salient for some groups than for others. The lower rate of Black/White intermarriage than Asian/White and Latino/White intermarriage suggests that the Black/White divide is more prominent as Asians and Latinos are perceived to fall in the non-Black category (Lee and Bean 2004, 237; Waters 2000).

8. As we have seen, some of the couples with children in this study decided to bring them up to identify with a minority ethnic group, for instance as African American (Judith and Walton), or to identify with a minority religion such as Judaism (James and Leila).

9. According to Jewish law, when Jewish children reach the age of thirteen they become responsible for their actions, and this new status is marked by a celebration of a Bar or Bat Mitzvah (English: *Son* (Bar) or *Daughter* (Bat) *of the commandments*). Prior to this, the child's parents are responsible for the child's adherence to Jewish law and tradition. After this rite of passage, children bear their own responsibility for Jewish ritual law, tradition, and ethics and are able to participate in all areas of Jewish community life.

Bibliography

Abdulrahim, Dima. 1993. "Defining Gender in a Second Exile: Palestinian Women in West Berlin." In *Migrant Women: Crossing Boundaries and Changing Identities*, edited by Gina Buijs, 52–75. Providence, RI: Berg.

Acker, Joan. 2006. "Inequality Regimes: Gender, Class, and Race in Organizations." *Gender & Society* 20 (4): 441–64.

Acker, Joan, Kate Barry, and Johanna Esseveld. 1983. "Objectivity and Truth: Problems in Doing Feminist Research." *Women's Studies International Forum* 6 (4): 423–35.

Ahmed, Sara. 2000. "Cultural Identities." In *Encyclopedia of Feminist Theories*, edited by Lorraine Code, 115–17. New York: Routledge.

Al-Ali, Nadje Sadig. 2007. *Iraqi Women: Untold Stories from 1948 to the Present*. London: Zed Books.

Alba, Richard D. 1990. *Ethnic Identity: The Transformation of White America*. New Haven: Yale University.

———. 1986. "Patterns of Interethnic Marriage among American Catholics." *Social Forces* 65 (1): 202–23.

Alcoff, Linda M. 2000. "Phenomenology, Post-structuralism, and Feminist Theory on the Concept of Experience." In *Feminist Phenomenology*, edited by Linda Fisher and L. Embree, 39–56. Dordrescht: Kluwer.

Alexander, Jeffrey C., and Steven Seidman. 1990. *Culture and Society: Contemporary Debates*. Cambridge University Press.

Allen, Katherine R., and Alexis J. Walker. 2000. "Qualitative Research." In *Close Relationships: A Sourcebook*, edited by Clyde Hendrick and Susan S. Hendrick, 19–29. Thousand Oaks, CA: Sage.

Allen, Sheila. 1998. "Identity: Feminist Perspectives on 'Race,' Ethnicity, and Nationality." In *Gender, Ethnicity, and Political Ideologies*, edited by Nickie Charles and Helen Hintjens, 46–64. London: Routledge.

Anderson, Benedict. 1991. *Imagined Communities: Reflections on the Origin and Spread of Nationalism*. 2d ed. London: Verso.

Anzaldua, Gloria. 1987. *Borderlands/La Frontera: The New Mestiza*. San Francisco: Spinsters/Aunt Lute.

Appiah, Kwame Anthony. 2005. *The Ethics of Identity*. Princeton: Princeton University Press.
———. 1996. *Color Conscious: The Political Morality of Race*. Princeton: Princeton University Press.
Archer, Louise. 2004. "Re/theorizing 'Difference' in Feminist Research." *Women's Studies International Forum* 27 (5): 459–73.
Arliss, Laurie P., and Deborah Borisoff, eds. 2001. *Women and Men Communicating: Challenges and Changes*. Prospect Heights, IL: Waveland Press.
Aron, Arthur, and Elaine N. Aron. 1997. "Self-Expansion and Including Other in the Self." In *Handbook of Personal Relationships*, 2d ed., edited by Steve Duck, 251–70. New York: Wiley.
Balnaves, Mark, Stephanie H. Donald, and Brian Shoesmith. 2009. *Media Theories and Approaches: Global Perspectives*. Brisbane: University of Queensland Press.
Barbara, Augustin. 1989. *Marriage Across Frontiers*. Philadelphia: Multilingual Matters.
Barron, Milton L. 1972. "Intergroup Aspects of Choosing a Mate." In *The Blending American: Patterns of Intermarriage*, edited by Milton L. Barron, 36–59. Chicago: Quadrangle Books.
Barvosa-Carter, Edwina. 2001. "Multiple Identity and Coalition Building: How Identity Differences Within Us Enable Radical Alliances Among Us." In *Forging Radical Alliances Across Difference: Coalition Politics for the New Millennium*, edited by Jill M. Bystydzienski and Steven P. Schacht, 21–34. Lanham, MD: Rowman & Littlefield.
Bell, Ann V. 2009. "'It's Way Out of My League': Low-Income Women's Experiences of Medicalized Infertility." *Gender & Society* 23 (5): 688–709.
Bem, Sandra L. 1993. *The Lenses of Gender: Transforming the Debate on Sexual Inequality*. New Haven: Yale University Press.
Berman, Louis Arthur. 1968. *Jews and Intermarriage: A Study in Personality and Culture*. New York: T. Yoseloff.
Bernard, Jessie. 1972. *The Future of Marriage*. New York: Bantam.
Bernstein, Mary. 2005. "Identity Politics." *Annual Review of Sociology* 31: 47–74.
Berscheid, Ellen, and Pamela Regan. 2005. *The Psychology of Interpersonal Relationships*. Upper Saddle River, NJ: Pearson Prentice Hall.
Bhabha, Homi. 1994. *The Location of Culture*. London: Routledge.
Bianchi, Suzanne M., Melissa M. Milkie, Liana C. Sayer, and John P. Robinson. 2000. "Is Anyone Doing the Housework? Trends in the Gender Division of Household Labor." *Social Forces* 79 (1): 191–228.
Biever, John L., Monte Bobele, and Mary-Wales North. 1998. "Therapy with Intercultural Couples: A Post-Modern Approach." *Counseling Psychology Quarterly* 11 (2): 181–88.
Bloom. Leslie R. 1998. *Under the Sign of Hope: Feminist Methodology and Narrative Interpretation*. Albany: State University of New York Press.

Blumstein, Phillip, and Pepper Schwartz. 1983. *American Couples: Money, Work, Sex.* New York: William Morrow.

Bondi, Liz, et al. 2002. *Subjectivities, Knowledges, and Feminist Geographies: The Subjects and Ethics of Social Research.* Lanham, MD: Rowman & Littlefield.

Bourdieu, Pierre. 1984. *Distinction: A Social Critique of the Judgment of Taste.* Cambridge: Harvard University Press.

Bratter, Jennifer L., and Rosalind B. King. 2008. "'But Will It Last?': Marital Instability Among Interracial and Same-Race Couples." *Family Relations* 57 (2): 160–71.

Breger, Rosemary, and Rosanna Hill. 1998. *Cross-cultural Marriage: Identity and Choice.* New York: Berg/Oxford International.

Brown, Christy, and Ayoub Farahyar. 1994. "Crossing Religious Lines in America." In *Inside the Mixed Marriage: Accounts of Changing Attitudes, Patterns, and Perceptions of Cross-Cultural and Interracial Marriages*, edited by Walton R. Johnson and D. Michael Warren, 173–92. Lanham, MD: University Press of America.

Browne, Kath. 2005. "Snowball Sampling: Using Social Networks to Research Non-Heterosexual Women." *International Journal of Social Research Methodology* 8 (1): 47–60.

Bucholtz, Mary, A. C. Liang, and Laurel A. Sutton, eds. 1999. *Reinventing Identities: The Gendered Self in Discourse.* New York: Oxford University Press.

Buijs, Gina, ed. 1993. *Migrant Women: Crossing Boundaries and Changing Identities.* Providence, RI: Berg.

Butler, Judith. 1998. *Bodies That Matter: On the Discursive Limits of "Sex."* New York: Routledge.

———. 1993. *Gender Trouble: Feminism and the Subversion of Identity.* New York: Routledge.

Bystydzienski, Jill M. 1995. *Women in Electoral Politics: Lessons from Norway.* Westport, CT: Praeger.

Bystydzienski, Jill M., and Steven P. Schacht. 2001. "Introduction." In *Forging Radical Alliances Across Difference: Coalition Politics for the New Millennium*, 1–17. Lanham, MD: Rowman & Littlefield.

Bystydzienski, Jill M., and Judy Aulette. 1990. "A Holistic Approach to Gender, Race, and Class Inequality." In *New Perspectives on Gender, Race and Class in Society*, edited by Audrey T. McCluskey. Women's Studies Occasional Papers, No. 4. Bloomington: Indiana University Press.

Calasanti, Toni M., and Kathleen F. Slevin. 2006. *Age Matters: Realigning Feminist Thinking.* New York: Taylor and Francis.

Calhoun, Craig. 1995. *Critical Social Theory: Culture, History, and the Challenge of Difference.* Oxford, UK: Blackwell.

Carlson, Robert G., Jichuan Wang, Harvey A Siegal, Russel S. Falk, and Jie Guo. 1994. "An Ethnographic Approach to Targeted Sampling: Problems and Solutions in AIDS Prevention Research Among Injection Drug and Crack-Cocaine Users." *Human Organization* 53 (3): 279–86.

Carpenter, Laura M. 2005. *Virginity Lost: An Intimate Portrait of First Sexual Experience.* New York: New York University Press.
Cerulo, Karen A. 1997. "Identity Construction: New Issues, New Directions." *Annual Review of Sociology* 23: 385–409.
Chancer, Lynn S., and Beverly Xaviera Watkins. 2006. *Gender, Race, and Class: An Overview.* Malden, MA: Blackwell.
Childs, Erica Chito. 2005. *Navigating Interracial Borders: Black-White Couples and Their Social Worlds.* New Brunswick: Rutgers University Press.
Clemetson, Lynette. 2000. "Love Without Borders." *Newsweek* (September 18): 62.
Code, Loraine. 1991. *What Can She Know? Feminist Theory and the Construction of Knowledge.* Ithaca: Cornell University Press.
Collier, Mary Jane. 2003. *Intercultural Alliances: Critical Transformations.* Thousand Oaks, CA: Sage.
Collins, Patricia Hill. 1995. "Symposium on West and Fenstermaker's 'Doing Difference.'" *Gender & Society* 9 (4): 491–94.
———. 1990. *Black Feminist Thought: Knowledge, Consciousness, and the Politics of Empowerment.* Boston: Unwin Hyman.
Coltrane, Scott. 2000. "Research on Household Labor: Modeling and Measuring the Social Embeddedness of Routine Family Work." *Journal of Marriage and the Family* 62 (4): 1208–33.
Connell, R. W. 1995. *Masculinites.* Berkeley and Los Angeles: University of California Press.
Constable, Nicole, ed. 2005. *Cross-Border Marriages: Gender and Mobility in Transnational Asia.* Philadelphia: University of Pennsylvania Press.
Coontz, Stephanie, ed. 2008. *American Families: A Multicultural Reader.* New York: Routledge.
Crohn, Joel. 1998. "Intercultural Couples." In *Re-visioning Family Therapy: Race, Culture, and Gender in Clinical Practice,* edited by Monica McGoldrick, 295–308. New York: Guilford Press.
Crompton, Rosemary. 1998. *Class and Stratification: An Introduction to Current Debates.* Malden, MA: Blackwell.
Curtis, Kristen Taylor, and Christopher G. Ellison. 2002. "Religious Heterogamy and Marital Conflict." *Journal of Family Issues* 23 (4): 551–76.
Cushman, Donald P., and Dudley D. Cahn. 1985. *Communication in Interpersonal Relationships.* Albany: State University of New York Press.
Davis, Kathy. 2007. *The Making of Our Bodies, Ourselves: How Feminism Travels Across Borders.* Durham: Duke University Press.
DeVault, Marjorie, and Glenda Gross. 2007. "Feminist Interviewing: Experience, Talk, and Knowledge." In *Handbook of Feminist Research: Theory and Praxis,* edited by Sharlene Nagy Hesse-Biber, 173–97. Thousand Oaks, CA: Sage.

Deutsch, Francine M. 2007. "Undoing Gender." *Gender & Society* 21 (1): 106–27.
Diggs, Nancy Brown. 2001. *Looking Beyond the Mask: When American Women Marry Japanese Men.* Albany: State University of New York Press.
Dindia, Kathryn, and Daniel J. Canary. 2006. *Sex Differences and Similarities in Communication: Critical Essays and Empirical Investigations of Sex and Gender in Interaction.* Mahwah, NJ: Erlbaum.
Dow, Bonnie J., and Julia T. Wood, eds. 2006. *The Sage Handbook of Gender and Communication.* Thousand Oaks, CA: Sage Publications.
Durodoye, Beth A., and Angela D. Coker. 2008. "Crossing Cultures in Marriage: Implications for Counseling African American/African Couples. *International Journal for the Advancement of Counseling* 30 (1): 25–37.
Edwards, Rosalind. 1990."Connecting Method and Epistemology: A White Woman Interviewing Black Women." *Women's Studies International Forum* 13: 477–90.
Eldridge, Natalie S., and Lucia.A. Gilbert. 1990. "Correlates of Relationship Satisfaction in Lesbian Couples." *Psychology of Women Quarterly* 14 (1): 43–62.
Elkin, Frederick. 1983. "Family, Socialization, and Ethnic Identity." In *The Canadian Family*, edited by K. Ishwaran, 145–58. Toronto: Gage.
Ellman, Israel. 1971. "Jewish Intermarriage in the United States." In *The Jewish Family*, edited by Benjamin Schlesinger, 36–52. Toronto: University of Toronto Press.
Erickson, Rebecca J. 1995. "The Importance of Authenticity for Self and Society." *Symbolic Interaction* 18 (2): 121–44.
Ferrante, Joan, and Prince Brown, Jr. 2001. *The Social Construction of Race and Ethnicity in the United States.* Upper Saddle River, NJ: Prentice Hall.
Fincham. Frank D. 2003. "Marital Conflict Correlates, Structure, and Context." *Current Directions in Psychological Science* 12 (1): 23–42.
Fiske, Susan T., and Shelley E. Taylor. 1991. *Social Cognition.* New York: McGraw-Hill.
Foeman, Anita K., and Teresa Nance. 1999. "From Miscegenation to Multiculturalism: Perceptions and Stages of Interracial Relationship Development." *Journal of Black Studies* 29 (4): 540–57.
Forry, Nicole D., Leigh A. Leslie, and Bethany L. Latiecq. 2007. "Marital Quality in Interracial Relationships: The Role of Sex Ideology and Perceived Fairness." *Journal of Family Issues* 28 (12): 1538–52.
Fountas, Angela Jane. 2005. *Waking Up American: Coming of Age Biculturally.* Emeryville, CA: Seal Press.
Frable, Deborrah E. S. 1997. "Gender, Racial, Ethnic, Sexual, and Class Identities." *Annual Review of Psychology* 48 (1): 139–62.
Frame, Marsha W. 2004. "The Challenge of Intercultural Marriage: Strategies for Pastoral Care." *Pastoral Psychology* 52 (3): 219–32.
Fredrickson, George M. 1988. *The Arrogance of Race: Historical Perspectives on Slavery, Racism, and Social Inequality.* Middletown: Wesleyan University Press.

Frye, Marilyn. 1983. "Oppression." In *The Politics of Reality: Essays in Feminist Theory*, edited by Marilyn Frye. Freedom, CA: The Crossing Press.

Fu, Vincent K. 2008. "Interracial-Interethnic Unions and Fertility in the United States." *Journal of Marriage and Family* 70 (3): 783–95.

Gaines, Stanley O., Jr. 1995. "Relationships Between Members of Cultural Minorities." In *Understanding Relationship Processes*, Vol. 6, edited by Julia T. Wood and Steve Duck, 51–88. Thousand Oaks, CA: Sage.

Gaines, Stanley O., Jr., and Christopher R. Agnew. 2003. "Relationship Maintenance in Intercultural Couples: An Interdependence Analysis." In *Maintaining Relationships Through Communication: Relational, Contextual, and Cultural Variations*, edited by Daniel J. Canary and Marianne Dainton, 23–53. Mahwah, NJ: Erlbaum.

Gaines, Stanley O., Jr., and William Ickes. 1997. "Perspectives on Interracial Relationships." In *Handbook of Personal Relationships*. 2nd ed., edited by Steve Duck, 197–220. New York: Wiley.

Gaines, Stanley O., Jr., and James H. Liu. 2000. "Multicultural/Multiracial Relationships." In *Close Relationships: A Sourcebook*, edited by Clyde Hendrick and Susan S. Hendrick, 97–110. Thousand Oaks, CA: Sage.

Gillis, John R. 1994. *Commemorations: The Politics of National Identity*. Princeton: Princeton University Press.

Glaser, Gabrielle. 1997. *Strangers to the Tribe: Portraits of Interfaith Marriage*. Boston: Houghton Mifflin.

Glauber, Rebecca. 2008. "Race and Gender in Families and at Work." *Gender & Society* 22 (1): 8–30.

Glazer, Nathan, and Daniel P. Moynihan. 1963. *Beyond the Melting Pot: The Negroes, Puerto Ricans, Jews, Italians, and Irish of New York City*. Cambridge: MIT Press.

Golebiowska, Ewa A. 2007. "The Contours and Etiology of Whites' Attitudes Toward Black-White Interracial Marriage." *Journal of Black Studies* 38 (2): 268–87.

Goodwin, Robin, and Duncan Cramer. 2002. *Inappropriate Relationships: The Unconventional, the Disapproved, and the Forbidden*. Mahwah, NJ: Erlbaum.

Gordon, Milton. 1964. *Assimilation in American Life: The Role of Race, Religion, and National Origins*. New York: Oxford University Press.

Grearson, Jessie Carroll, and Lauren B. Smith. 2001. *Love in a Global Village: A Celebration of Intercultural Families in the Midwest*. Iowa City: University of Iowa Press.

Grearson, Jessie Carroll, and Lauren B. Smith, eds. 1995. *Swaying: Essays on Intercultural Love*. Iowa City: University of Iowa Press.

Griswold, Wendy. 1992. "The Writing on the Mud Wall: Nigerian Novels and the Imaginary Village." *American Sociological Review* 57 (6): 709–24.

Gullickson, Aaron. 2006. "Education and Black-White Interracial Marriage." *Demography* 43 (4): 673–89.

Hall, Christine C. Iijima. 1992. "Please Choose One: Ethnic Identity Choices for Biracial Individuals." In *Racially Mixed People in America*, edited by Maria P. P. Root, 239–49. Newbury Park, CA: Sage.
Hall, Stuart. 1996. "Introduction: Who Needs Identity?" In *Questions of Cultural Identity*, ed. Stuart Hall and Paul du Gay, 1–17. Thousand Oaks, CA: Sage.
Hall, Stuart, and Paul du Gay, eds. 1996. *Questions of Cultural Identity*. Thousand Oaks, CA: Sage.
Hammonds, Evelynn M. 2005. "Straw Men and Their Followers: The Return of Biological Race." Online forum on race and genomics, the Social Science Research Council (SSRC), http://raceandgenomics.ssrc.org.
Hammonds, Evelynn M., et al. 2005. "The Use of Race Variables in Genetic Studies of Complex Traits and the Goal of Reducing Health Disparities." *American Psychologist* 60 (1): 77–103.
Haney-Lopez, Ian F. 1995. "The Social Construction of Race." In *Critical Race Theory*, edited by Richard Delgado, 191–203. Philadelphia: Temple University Press.
Haraway, Donna. 1991. "Situated Knowledges: The Science Question in Feminism and the Privilege of Partial Perspective." In *Simians, Cyborgs, and Women*, 183–202. London: Free Association Books.
Harding, Sandra. 1991. *Whose Science, Whose Knowledge? Thinking from Women's Lives*. Milton Keynes, UK: Open University Press.
Hendrick, Clyde, and Susan S. Hendrick, eds. 2000. *Close Relationships: A Sourcebook*. Thousand Oaks, CA: Sage.
Hesse-Biber, Sharlene Nagy, and Michelle L. Yaiser, eds. 2004. *Feminist Perspectives on Social Research*. New York: Oxford University Press.
Heyman, Richard E., Ashley Hunt-Martorano, Jill Malik, and Amy M. Smith Slep. 2009. "Desired Change in Couples: Gender Differences and Effects on Communication." *Journal of Family Psychology* 23 (4): 474–84.
hooks, bell. 2000. *Where We Stand: Class Matters*. New York: Routledge.
———. 1981. *Ain't I a Woman: Black Women and Feminism*. Boston: South End Press.
Howard, Judith A. 2000. "Social Psychology of Identities." *Annual Review of Sociology* 26: 367–93.
Hurtado, Aida. 2003. *Voicing Chicana Feminism: Young Women Speak Out on Sexuality and Identity*. New York: New York University Press.
———. 1997. "Understanding Multiple Group Identities: Inserting Women into Cultural Transformation." *Journal of Social Issues* 53 (2): 299–328.
Hutter, Mark. 1990. "Introduction." *Journal of Comparative Family Studies* 21 (2): 143–50.
Ibrahim, Farah A., and David O. Schroeder. 1990. "Cross-Cultural Couple Counseling." *Journal of Comparative Family Studies* 21 (2): 193–205.
Ichiyama, Michael, Edward McQuarrie, and Kristine Ching. 1996. "Contextual Influences on Ethnic Identity Among Hawaiian Students in the Mainland United States." *Journal of Cross-Cultural Psychology* 27 (4): 458–75.

Jacobson, Cardell K., and Bryan Johnson. 2006. "Interracial Friendship and African American Attitudes About Interracial Marriage." *Journal of Black Studies* 36 (4): 570–84.

Johnson, Judith, and Walton Johnson. 1994. "Differences Can Be Strengths." In *Inside the Mixed Marriage: Accounts of Changing Attitudes, Patterns, and Perceptions of Cross-Cultural and Interracial Marriages,* edited by Walton R. Johnson and D. Michael Warren, 193–201. Lanham, MD: University Press of America.

Johnson, Walton R., and D. Michael Warren, eds. 1994. *Inside the Mixed Marriage: Accounts of Changing Attitudes, Patterns, and Perceptions of Cross-cultural and Interracial Marriages.* Lanham, MD: University Press of America.

Judd, Eleanore Parelman. 1990. "Intermarriage and the Maintenance of Religio-Ethnic Identity. A Case Study: The Denver Jewish Community." *Journal of Comparative Family Studies* 21 (2): 251–68.

Kalmijn, Matthijs. 1998. "Intermarriage and Homogamy: Causes, Patterns, Trends." *Annual Review of Sociology* 24: 395–421.

Kaplan, Jane. 2004. *Interfaith Families: Personal Stories of Jewish-Christian Intermarriage.* Westport, CT: Praeger.

Kellner, Judith. 2009. "Gender Perspective in Cross-Cultural Couples." *Clinical Social Work Journal* 37 (3): 224–29.

Kennedy, Randall. 2004. *Interracial Intimacies: Sex, Marriage, Identity, and Adoption.* New York: Vintage.

Kennedy, Ruby Jo Reeves. 1952. "Single or Triple Melting Pot? Intermarriage in New Haven, 1870–1950." *The American Journal of Sociology* 58 (1): 56–59.

King, Deborah. 1990. "Multiple Jeopardy, Multiple Consciousness: The Context of a Black Feminist Ideology." In *Black Women in America: Social Science Perspectives,* edited by Michelene R. Malson et al. Chicago: University of Chicago Press.

Kirkpatrick, Martha. 1989. "Middle Age and the Lesbian Experience." *Women's Studies Quarterly* 17 (1/2): 87–96.

Kitch, Sally L. 2009. *The Specter of Sex: Gendered Foundations of Racial Formation in the United States.* Albany: State University of New York Press.

Kornblum, William, and Carolyn D. Smith. 1996. *Introduction to Sociology.* New York: Macmillan.

Kruks, Sonia. 2001. *Retrieving Experience: Subjectivity and Recognition in Feminist Politics.* Ithaca: Cornell University Press.

Kurdek, Lawrence A. 2003. "Differences between Gay and Lesbian Cohabiting Couples." *Journal of Social and Personal Relationships* 20 (4): 411–36.

Kurdek, Lawrence A., and John P. Schmitt. 1987. "Partner Homogamy in Married, Heterosexual Cohabiting, Gay, and Lesbian Couples. *Journal of Sex Research* 23 (1): 212–32.

———. 1986. "Relationship Quality of Partners in Heterosexual Married, Heterosexual Cohabiting, and Gay and Lesbian Relationships." *Journal of Personality and Social Psychology* 51 (4): 711–20.

La Ferla, Ruth. 2003. "Generation E. A.: Ethnically Ambiguous." *The New York Times* (December 28): 9: 1, 9.

Lazerwitz, Bernard. 1995. "Jewish-Christian Marriages and Conversions, 1971 and 1990." *Sociology of Religion* 56 (4): 433–43.

Lee, Jennifer, and Frank D. Bean. 2004. "America's Changing Color Lines: Immigration, Race/Ethnicity, and Multiracial Identification." *Annual Review of Sociology* 30: 221–42.

Lee, Raymond M. 1994. *Mixed and Matched: Interreligious Courtship and Marriage in Northern Ireland.* Lanham, MD: University Press of America.

Lee, Sharon, and Keiko Yamanaka. 1990. "Patterns of Asian American Intermarriage and Marital Assimilation." *Journal of Comparative Family Studies* 21 (2): 287–305.

Lenz, Brooke. 2004. "Postcolonial Fiction and the Outsider Within: Towards a Literary Practice of Feminist Standpoint Theory." *NWSA Journal* 16 (2): 98–120.

Leslie, Leigh A., and Bethany L. Letiecq. 2004. "Marital Quality of African American and White Partners in Interracial Couples." *Personal Relationships* 11 (4): 559–74.

Levine, Gene N., and Colbert Rhodes. 1981. *The Japanese American Community: A Three-Generation Study.* New York: Praeger.

Litt, Jacquelyn. 2000. *Medicalized Motherhood: Perspectives from the Lives of African American and Jewish Women.* New Brunswick: Rutgers University Press.

Lopes, Claudia S., Laura C. Rodrigues, and Rosely Sichieri. 1996. "The Lack of Selection Bias in a Snowball Sampled Case-Control Study on Drug Abuse." *International Journal of Epidemiology* 25 (6): 1267–70.

Lorber, Judith. 2005. *Gender Inequality: Feminist Theories and Politics.* Los Angeles: Roxbury.

Lugones, Maria. 2005. "From Within Germinative Stasis: Creating Active Subjectivity, Resistant Agency." In *Entre Mundos/Among Worlds: New Perspectives on Gloria Anzaldua,* edited by AnaLouise Keating, 85–100. New York: Palgrave Macmillan.

Lyman, Scott M., and William A. Douglas. 1973. "Ethnicity: Strategies for Collective and Individual Impression Management." *Social Research* 40 (3): 344–65.

Mackey, Richard A., Bernard O'Brien, and Euleen Mackey. 1997. *Gay and Lesbian Couples: Voices from Lasting Relationships.* Westport, CT: Praeger.

Mayer, Egon. 1985. *Love and Tradition: Marriage Between Jews and Christians.* New York: Plenum Press.

McCall, George J., and J. L. Simmons. 1996. *Identities and Interactions.* New York: Free Press.

McCarthy, Kate. 2007. "Pluralist Family Values: Domestic Strategies for Living with Religious Difference." *The Annals of the American Academy of Political and Social Science* 612 (1): 188–208.

McDermott, John F., Jr., and Charles Fukunaga. 1977. "Intercultural Family Interaction Patterns." In *Adjustments in Intercultural Marriage,* edited by W. S. Tseng, John F. McDermott Jr., and Thomas W. Marezki, 81–92. Honolulu: University Press of Hawaii.

McGinity, Karen R. 2008. *Still Jewish: A History of Women and Intermarriage in America*. New York: New York University Press.

McMaster, Carrie. 2005. "Negotiating Paradoxical Spaces: Women, Disabilities, and the Experience of Nepantla." In *Entre Mundos/Among Worlds: New Perspectives on Gloria Anzaldua*, edited by AnaLouise Keating, 101–6. New York: Palgrave Macmillan.

McNamara, Robert P., Maria Tempenis, and Beth Walton. 1999. *Crossing the Line: Interracial Couples in the South*. Westport, CT: Greenwood Press.

Medding, Peter Y. 1992. *Jewish Identity in Conversionary and Mixed Marriages*. New York: American Jewish Committee, Institute of Human Relations.

Mediatore, Shari Stone. 2003. *Reading Across Borders: Storytelling and Knowledge of Resistance*. New York: Palgrave Macmillan.

Merton, Robert K. 1941. "Intermarriage and the Social Structure." *Psychiatry* 4: 361–74.

Millman, Marcia. 1991. *Warm Hearts and Cold Cash: The Intimate Dynamics of Families and Money*. New York: Free Press.

Monahan, Thomas. 1973. "Some Dimensions of Interreligious Marriages in the United States." *Social Forces* (December): 195–203.

Moya, Paula M. L. 2001. "Chicana Feminism and Postmodernist Theory." *Signs* 26 (2): 441–83.

———. 1997. "Postmodernism, 'Realism,' and the Politics of Identity." In *Feminist Genealogies, Colonial Legacies, Democratic Futures*, edited by M. Jacqui Alexander and Chandra Talpade Mohanty, 125–50. New York: Routledge.

Muhsam, Hanah. 1990. "Social Distance and Asymmetry in Intermarriage Patterns." *Journal of Comparative Family Studies* 21 (3): 307–24.

Murguia, Edward, and W. Parker Frisbie. 1977. "Trends in Mexican American Intermarriage: Recent Findings in Perspective." *Social Science Quarterly* 58 (December): 374–89.

Narayan, Uma. 2000. "Undoing the 'Package Picture' of Cultures." *Signs: Journal of Women in Culture and Society* 25 (4): 1083–86.

National Public Radio (NPR). 2009. "Mixed Race Americans Picture a 'Blended Nation.'" Weekend Edition, November 8.

National Survey of Families and Households. 2005. Madison: University of Wisconsin Center for Demography. http//www.ssc.wisc.edu/nsfh/ (accessed July 12, 2008).

O'Brien, Eileen. "The Political is Personal: The Influence of White Supremacy on White Antiracists' Personal Relationships." In *White Out: The Continuing Significance of Racism*, edited by Ashley W. Doane and Eduardo Bonilla-Silva, 253–67. New York: Routledge.

Okin, Susan Moller. 1989. *Justice, Gender, and the Family*. New York: Basic Books.

Ollilainen, Marjukka, and Toni Calasanti. 2007. "Metaphors at Work: Maintaining the Salience of Gender in Self-Managing Teams." *Gender & Society* 21 (1): 5–27.

Omi, Michael, and Howard Winant. 1986. *Racial Formation in the United States*. New York: Routledge & Kegan Paul.

Orbe, Mark P., and Tina M. Harris. 2001. *Interracial Communication: Theory into Practice*. Belmont, CA: Wadsworth/Thomson Learning.

Ortega, Mariana. 2005. "Apertures of In-Betweeness, of Selves in the Middle." In *Entre Mundos/Among Worlds: New Perspectives on Gloria Anzaldua*, edited by AnaLouise Keating, 77–84. New York: Palgrave Macmillan.

Paget, Marianne. 1983. "Experience and Knowledge." *Human Studies* 6: 67–90.

Patterson, Carla J. 1995. "Families of the Lesbian Baby Boom: Parents' Division of Labor and Children's Adjustment." *Developmental Psychology* 31 (1): 115–23.

Peplau, Letitia Anne, and Leah R. Spalding. 2000. "The Close Relationships of Lesbians, Gay Men, and Bisexuals." In *Close Relationships: A Sourcebook*, edited by Clyde Hendrick and Susan S. Hendrick, 111–23. Thousand Oaks, CA: Sage.

Piskacek, V., and Michael Golub. 1973. "Children of Interracial Marriages." In *Interracial Marriage: Expectations and Realities*, edited by Irving R. Stuart and Lawrence E. Abt, 53–61. New York: Grossman.

Ragsdale, Donald J. 1996. "Gender, Satisfaction Level, and the Use of Relational Maintenance Strategies in Marriage." *Communication Monographs* 63 (4): 354–69.

Reay, Diane. 2004. "Rethinking Social Class: Qualitative Perspectives on Class and Gender." In *Feminist Perspectives on Social Research*, edited by Sharlene Nagy Hesse-Biber and Michelle L. Yaiser, 140–54. New York: Oxford University Press.

Reinharz, Shulamit. 1992. "Feminist Interview Research." In *Feminist Methods in Social Research*, 18–45. New York: Oxford University Press.

Reiter, Michael J., and Christina B. Gee. 2008. "Open Communication and Partner Support in Intercultural and Interfaith Romantic Relationships: A Relational Maintenance Approach." *Journal of Social and Personal Relationships* 25 (4): 539–59.

Romano, Dugan. 1988. *Intercultural Marriage: Promises and Pitfalls*. Yarmouth, ME: Intercultural Press.

Romano, Renee C. 2003. *Race Mixing: Black-White Marriage in Postwar America*. Cambridge: Harvard University Press.

Root, Maria P. P. 2001. *Love's Revolution: Interracial Marriage*. Philadelphia: Temple University Press.

———, ed. 1992. *Racially Mixed People in America*. Newbury Park, CA: Sage.

Rosenblatt, Paul C., Teri A. Karis, and Richard Powell. 1995. *Multiracial Couples: Black and White Voices*. Thousand Oaks, CA: Sage.

Rosenblum, Karen E., and Toni-Michelle C. Travis. 2006. *The Meaning of Difference: American Constructions of Race, Sex and Gender, Social Class, and Sexual Orientation*. Boston: McGraw-Hill.

Rosenfeld, Michael J. 2007. *The Age of Independence: Interracial Unions, Same-Sex Unions, and the Changing American Family.* Cambridge: Harvard University Press.

Rowe, Amy Carillo, and Adela C. Licona. 2005. "Moving Locations: The Politics of Identities in Motion." *NWSA Journal* 17 (2): 11–14.

Rubin, Lilian B. 1995. *Families on the Fault Line: America's Working Class Speaks About the Family, the Economy, and Ethnicity.* New York: Harper Collins.

———. 1976. *Worlds of Pain: Life in a Working-Class Family.* New York: Basic Books.

Rusbult, C. E., and B. P. Buunk. 1993. "Commitment Processes in Close Relationships: An Interdependence Analysis." *Journal of Social and Personal Relationships* 10: 175–204.

Scott, Joan W. 1992. "Experience." In *Feminists Theorize the Political*, edited by Judith Butler and Joan W. Scott, 22–40. New York: Routledge.

Seidman, Steven. 2002. *Beyond the Closet: The Transformation of Gay and Lesbian Life.* New York: Routledge.

Seshagiri, Urmila. 2003. "At the Crossroads of Two Empires: Mira Nair's *Mississippi Massa* and the Limits of Hybridity." *Journal of Asian American Studies* 6 (2): 177–98.

Sillars, Alan, Linda J. Roberts, and Tim Dun. 2000. "Cognition During Marital Conflict: The Relationship of Thought and Talk." *Journal of Social and Personal Relationships* 17 (4–5): 479–502.

Skegg, Beverley. 2004. *Class, Self, Culture.* New York: Routledge.

Smith, Barbara. 1993. "Homophobia: Why Bring It Up?" In *The Lesbian and Gay Studies Reader,* edited by Henry Abelove, Michile Aina Barale, and David Halperin. New York: Routledge.

Smith, Dorothy E. 1990. *Texts, Facts, and Femininity: Exploring the Relations of Ruling.* New York: Routledge.

———. 1987. *The Everyday World as Problematic: A Feminist Sociology.* Boston: Northern University Press.

Smith, Reger C. 1996. *Two Cultures, One Marriage: Premarital Counseling for Mixed Marriages.* Berrien Springs: Andrews University Press.

Smith, Sidonie, and JuliaWatson. 2001. *Reading Autobiography: A Guide for Interpreting Life Narratives.* Minneapolis: University of Minnesota Press.

Spickard, Paul R. 1989. *Mixed Blood: Intermarriage and Ethnic Identity in Twentieth-Century America.* Madison: University of Wisconsin Press.

Spillman, Lyn. 1997. *Nation and Commemoration: Creating National Identities in the United States and Australia.* New York: Cambridge University Press.

Staples, Robert, and L. Boulin Johnson. 1993. *Black Families at the Crossroads: Challenges and Prospects.* San Francisco: Jossey-Bass.

Steinbugler, Amy C. 2005. "Visibility as Privilege and Danger: Heterosexual and Same-Sex Interracial Intimacy in the 21st Century." *Sexualities* 8 (4): 425–43.

Bibliography

Stephan, Cookie White. 1992. "Mixed Heritage Individuals: Ethnic Identity and Trait Characteristics." In *Racially Mixed People in America*, edited by Maria P. P. Root, 50–63. Newbury Park, CA: Sage.

Stewart, Lea P., et al. 2003. *Communication and Gender*. 4th ed. Boston: Allyn and Bacon.

Strong, Bryan, Christine DeVault, and Barbara W. Sayad. 1998. *The Marriage and Family Experience: Intimate Relationships in a Changing Society*. Belmont, CA: Wadsworth.

Stryker, Sheldon. 1980. *Symbolic Interactionism: A Social Structural Version*. Menlo Park, CA: Benjamin/Cummings.

Stuart, Irving R., and Lawrence E. Abt, eds. 1973. *Interracial Marriage: Expectations and Realities*. New York: Grossman.

Tajfel, Henri. 1981. *Human Groups and Social Categories: Studies in Social Psychology*. London: Cambridge University Press.

Takagi, Dana. 1996. "Maiden Voyage: Excursion into Sexuality and Identity Politics in Asian America." In *Asian American Sexualities: Dimensions of the Gay and Lesbian Experience*, edited by Russell Leong. New York: Routledge.

Tannen, Deborah. 1996. *Gender and Discourse*. New York: Oxford University Press.

———. 1990. *You Just Don't Understand: Women and Men in Conversation*. New York: Ballantyne Books.

Tartakov, Carlie, and Gary Tartakov. 1994. "Interracial or Cross-Cultural?" In *Inside the Mixed Marriage: Accounts of Changing Attitudes, Patterns, and Perceptions of Cross-Cultural and Interracial Marriages*, edited by Walton R. Johnson and D. Michael Warren, 147–54. Lanham, MD: University Press of America.

Tauber, Mike, Pamela Singh, and Alan Goodman. 2009. *Blended Nation: Portraits and Interviews of Mixed-Race America*. San Francisco: Chanel Photographics.

Taylor, Verta, and Nancy E. Whittier. 1992. "Collective Identity in Social Movement Communities: Lesbian Feminist Mobilization." In *Frontiers in Social Movement Theory*, edited by A. D. Morris and C. M. Mueller, 104–29. New Haven: Yale University Press.

Thornton, Michael C. 1992. "The Quiet Immigration: Foreign Spouses of U.S. Citizens, 1945–1985." In *Racially Mixed People in America*, edited by Maria P. P. Root, 64–76. Newbury Park, CA: Sage.

Troy, Adam B., Jamie Lewis-Smith, and Jean-Philippe Laurenceau. 2006. "Interracial and Intraracial Romantic Relationships: The Search for Differences in Satisfaction, Conflict, and Attachment Style." *Journal of Social and Personal Relationships* 23 (1): 65–80.

U.S. Census Bureau. 2008a. Married Couples by Race and Hispanic Origin of Spouses: 1970–2006; Table 59. *Statistical Abstract of the United States*. Lanham, MD: Berman Press.

———. 2008b. Interracial Married Couples, 1980–2006. *Statistical Abstract of the United States*. Information Please® Database, Pearson Education. http://www.infoplease.com/ipa/A0922160.html.

Vosburgh, Miriam G., and Richard N. Juliani. 1990. "Contrasts in Ethnic Family Patterns: The Irish and the Italians." *Journal of Comparative Family Studies* 21 (2): 269–86.

Wajcman, Judy. 1983. *Women in Control: Dilemmas of a Workers' Cooperative*. New York: St. Martin's Press.

Walter, Roland. 2003. *Narrative Identities: (Inter)Cultural In-Betweenness in the Americas*. New York: P. Lang.

Wanzo, Rebecca. 2009. *The Suffering Will Not Be Televised*. Albany: State University of New York Press.

Ward, Jane. 2004. "'Not All Differences Are Created Equal': Multiple Jeopardy in a Gendered Organization." *Gender & Society* 18 (1): 82–102.

Waters, Mary C. 2000. "Multiple Ethnicities and Identity in the United States." In *We Are a People*, edited by Paul R. Spickard and William J. Burroughs, 23–40. Philadelphia: Temple University Press.

Weber, Lynn. 2004. "A Conceptual Framework for Understanding Race, Class, Gender, and Sexuality." In *Feminist Perspectives on Social Research*, edited by Sharlene Nagy Hesse-Biber and Michelle L. Yaiser, 121–39. New York: Oxford University Press.

West, Candace, and Sarah Fernstermaker. 1995. "Doing Difference." *Gender & Society* 9 (1): 8–37.

Wilkerson, Isabel. 1991. "Continuing Lack of Acceptance of Interracial Marriage." *Journal of Marriage and the Family* 53 (November): 904–12.

Wood, Julia T. 2005. *Gendered Lives: Communication, Gender, and Culture*. Belmont, CA: Wadsworth/Thomson Learning.

———. 1996. *Gendered Relationships*. Mountain View, CA: Mayfield.

———. 1993. "Engendered Relationships: Interaction, Caring, Power, and Responsibility in Close Relationships." In *Processes in Close Relationships: Contexts of Close Relationships*, Vol 3, edited by Steve Duck, 26–54. Beverly Hills, CA: Sage.

Yancey, George, and Richard Lewis Jr. 2009. *Interracial Families: Current Concepts and Controversies*. New York: Routledge.

Yuval-Davis, Nira. 1997. *Gender and Nation*. Thousand Oaks, CA: Sage.

Zhang, Yuanting, and Jennifer Van Hook. 2009. "Marital Dissolution Among Interracial Couples." *Journal of Marriage and the Family* 71 (1): 95–107.

Zinn, Maxine Baca, and Bonnie Dill. 1996. "Theorizing Difference from Multiracial Feminism." *Feminist Studies* 22 (2): 321–31.

Zinn, Maxine Baca, and D. Stanley Eitzen, eds. 1996. *Diversity in Families*. New York: Harper Collins.

Index

Abdulrahim, Dima, 6
Acker, Joan, 189n2
Acker, Joan, Kate Barry, and Johanna Essevold, 177
Ahmed, Sara, 47, 48, 49
Alba, Richard, 7, 46, 71
Alcoff, Linda, 182
Alexander, Jeffrey, and Steven Seidman, 189n3
Allen, Katherine, and Alexis Walker, 10
Allen, Sheila, 49
Anderson, Benedict, 49
Anzaldua, Gloria, 10, 50
Appiah, Kwame Anthony, 192n5
Archer, Louise, 8
Arliss, Laurie, and Deborah Borisoff, 152
Aron, Arthur, and Elaine Aron, 138
Assimilation, 7, 46

Balnaves, Mark, Stephanie Donald, and Brian Shoesmith, 169
Barbara, Augustin, 6
Barron, Milton, 6, 46, 71
Barvosa-Carter, Edwina, 9, 82
Bell, Ann, 8
Bem, Sandra, 49
Berman, Louis Arthur, 2, 127
Bernard, Jessie, 13, 45
Bernstein, Mary, 47, 48, 50, 71

Berscheid, Ellen, and Pamela Regan, 138
Bhabha, Homi, 10, 50, 75, 172
Bianchi, Suzanne, et al, 103
Biever, John, Monte Bobele, and Mary-Wales North, 189n1
Bloom, Leslie, 8
Blumstein, Phillip, and Pepper Schwartz, 154, 189n4, 191n2
Bondi, Liz, et al., 8
Bourdieu, Pierre, 198n3
Bratter, Jennifer, and Rosalind King, 2, 7, 19, 165–66
Breger, Rosemary, and Rosanna Hill, 2, 3, 6, 82
Brown, Christy, and Ayoub Farahyar, 11, 88–90, 98–99, 105, 106
Browne, Kath, 12, 190n11
Bucholtz, Mary, A. C. Liang, and Laurel Sutton, 49
Buijs, Gina, 6
Butler, Judith, 49, 189n2
Bystydzienski, Jill, 190n11
Bystydzienski, Jill, and Judy Aulette, 9
Bystydzienski, Jill, and Steven Schacht, 168

Calasanti, Toni, and Kathleen Slevin, 82
Calhoun, Craig, 48, 71
Carlson, Robert, et al., 12, 190n11

Index

Carpenter, Laura, 8, 177, 190n13
Cerulo, Karen, 48
Chancer, Lynn, and Beverly Xaviera Watkins, 8, 9, 189n2, 189n3
Children, of intercultural couples, 11, 118–19, 172–74
Childs, Erica Chito, 2, 7, 62, 112, 166, 190n11, 190n13, 191n3
Class, 4, 82–96, 108–9. *See also* Conflict, management in financial matters
Clemetson, Lynette, 1, 46
Code, Loraine, 182
Collier, Mary Jane, 189n1
Collins, Patricia Hill, 8, 9, 182
Coltrane, Scott, 103
"Compensatory hypogamy," 6
Conflict: accommodation strategies, 139, 168; over family relations, 144–52; management in financial matters, 139–44
Connell, R. W., 49
Constable, Nicole, 54
Coontz, Stephanie, 45, 46, 172, 173, 191n2
Crohn, Joel, 189n1
Crompton, Rosemary, 189n3
Cultural differences, recognition of, 51–61
Culture: definition, 2; and identity, 49; intersection with religion, 133–36
Curtis, Kristen, and Christopher Ellison, 2, 166
Cushman, Donald, and Dudley Cahn, 138

Davis, Kathy, 182
Deutsch, Francine, 82
DeVault, Marjorie, and Glenda Gross, 177, 179
Diggs, Nancy Brown, 7, 13, 19, 46, 53, 82, 190n13

Dindia, Kathryn, and Daniel Canary, 152
Domestic partnerships, 8, 45
Dow, Bonnie, and Julia Wood, 152
Durodoye, Beth, and Angela Coker, 62, 138

Edwards, Rosalind, 179
Egalitarian gender roles, 105–8
Eldridge, Natalie, and Lucia Gilbert, 154
Elkin, Frederick, 48
Ellman, Israel, 7
Erickson, Rebecca, 50
Ethical concerns, 180
Ethnicity, 5
Exogamous partnerships, 7, 138, 158, 191ch5n1
Experience, 7, 8, 182; and memory, 182–83

Family structure demographic changes, 1
Feminist scholarship on difference, 8–10; intersectionality, 9; social locations that resist categorization, 10; socially constructed categories, 9
Ferrante, Joan, and Prince Brown, Jr., 5, 9
Financial conflict, 82–96, 139–44
Fincham, Frank, 191n2
Fiske, Susan, and Shelley Taylor, 138
Foeman, Anita, and Teresa Nance, 125, 191n4
Forry, Nicole, Leigh Leslie, and Bethany Latiecq, 2, 7
Fountas, Angela Jane, 10, 172, 173
Frable, Deborrah, 50
Frame, Marsha, 7, 166
Frederickson, George, 5
Frye, Marilyn, 10
Fu, Vincent, 2

Index

Gaines, Stanley O. Jr., 46
Gaines, Stanley O. Jr., and Christopher Agnew, 189n1
Gaines, Stanley O. Jr., and William Ickes, 6, 166
Gaines, Stanley O. Jr., and James Liu, 7, 47, 126, 138
Gender, 4, 96–103; differences in communication, 152–54
Gillis, John, 49
Glaser, Gabrielle, 2, 127
Glauber, Rebecca, 82
Glazer, Nathan, and Daniel Moynihan, 192n6
Golebiowska, Ewa, 166
Goodwin, Robin, and Duncan Cramer, 165
Gordon, Milton, 6, 7, 46, 71
Grearson, Jessie, and Lauren Smith, 2, 7, 45, 46
Griswold, Wendy, 49
Gullickson, Aaron, 2

Hall, Stuart, 49, 50, 173
Hall, Stuart, and Paul du Gay, 47
Hammonds, Evelynn, 192n5
Hammonds, Evelynn et al., 192n5
Haney-Lopez, Ian, 5
Haraway, Donna, 182
Harding, Sandra, 182
Hendrick, Clyde, and Susan Hendrick, 138
Hesse-Biber, Charlene Nagy, and Michelle Yaiser, 8
Heyman, Richard et al., 152
hooks, bell, 108–9, 189n3, 191n1
Howard, Judith, 47, 48, 50
Hurtado, Aida, 9, 47, 48, 82
Hutter, Mark

Ibrahim, Farah, and David Schroeder, 6
Ichiyama, Michael, et al., 64

Identity, 46–79; "borderland identities," 50; postmodern approach, 49–50; social constructionist approach, 49; traditional or essentialist approach, 48–49; transformation, 46
Intercultural couples: definition, 1, 2, 4, 10, 189n1; with children, 11, 118–19, 172–74; demographics of study sample, 18–19; experiences of, 7, 8, 182; feminist study of, 8–10; as form of assimilation, 7, 46; negative portrayals, 6–7; representation in popular culture, 169–72; statistics, 1; sympathetic views, 7
Interfaith marriage, 2, *See also* Religion
Intergroup couples, 6; form of assimilation, 7; negative portrayals, 6–7; sympathetic views, 7
International couples, 2, 51
Interracial couples, 2

Johnson, Judith, and Walton Johnson, 11, 111, 117–19
Johnson, Walton, and D. Michael Warren, 2, 7
Judd, Eleanore Parelman, 46, 173

Kalmijn, Matthijs, 1, 6, 166, 167
Kaplan, Jane, 2, 127
Kellner, Judith, 7
Kennedy, Randall, 2
Kennedy, Ruby Jo Reeves, 7
Kirkpatrick, Martha, 154
Kitch, Sally, 8
Kornblum, William, and Carolyn Smith, 190ch.1n1
Kruks, Sonia, 182
Kurdek, Lawrence, 154
Kurdek, Lawrence, and John Smith, 154

[209]

Index

La Ferla, Ruth, 172
Lazerwitz, Bernard, 2
Lee, Jennifer, and Frank Bean, 1, 165, 172, 173, 191ch.4n2, 192n4, 192n7
Lee, Raymond, 2
Lee, Sharon, and Keiko Yamanka, 6
Lenz, Brooke, 10
Leslie, Leigh, and Bethany Letiecq, 7
Levine, Gene, and Colbert Rhodes, 6, 7
Litt, Jacquelyn, 8, 190n13
Lopes, Claudia, Laura Rodrigues, and Rosely Sichieri, 12
Lorber, Judith, 189n2
Lugones, Maria, 50
Lyman, Scott, and William Douglas, 46

Mackey, Richard, Bernard O'Brien, and Euleen Mackey, 155
Mayer, Egon, 127
McCall, George, and J. L. Simmons, 47
McCarthy, Kate, 46, 127
McDermott, John F. Jr., and Charles Fukunaga, 49
McGinity, Karen, 2
McMaster, Carrie, 50
McNamara, Robert, Maria Tempenis, and Beth Walton, 2, 19, 82, 112, 190n13
Mediatore, Shari Stone, 182
Medding, Peter, 2
Merton, Robert, 6
Millman, Marcia, 191n2
Minority group partners, 71
Mississippi Masala, 170
Monahan, Thomas, 2
Moya, Paula, 9, 10, 182
Muhsam, Hanah, 6
Muguia, Edward, and W. Parker Frisbie, 7

Nair, Mira, 170
Narayan, Uma, 3, 49, 162

National Public Radio, 172, 192n4
National Survey of Families and Households, 103
Nationality, 4, 17
Negotiations of difference, 2

O'Brien, Eileen, 190n3
Okin, Susan Moller, 152
Ollilainen, Marjuka, and Toni Calasanti, 82
Omi, Michael, and Howard Winant, 5
Orbe, Mark, and Tina Harris, 64, 125, 138, 152
Ortega, Mariana, 50

Paget, Marianne, 179
Patterson, Carla, 105
Peplau, Leticia Anne, and Leah Spalding, 105
Piskacek, V., and Michael Golub, 49

Qualitative methods, 10; analysis of interview data, 14; in-depth interviews, 10, 13, 177

Race, 4, 111, 112–17; responses to racism, 125–27; and sexual orientation, 121–24
Ragsdale, Donald, 152
Reay, Diane, 191n1
Reinharz, Shulamit, 177
Reiter, Michael, and Christina Gee, 7, 166, 198n1
Relational identity, 46, 75–78, 138–39
Religion, 4, 111, 127–36
Romano, Dugan, 2
Romano, Renee, 2
Root, Maria, 2, 7, 46, 54, 62, 82, 172
Rosenblatt, Paul, Teri Karis, and Richard Powell, 2, 46, 190n11, 190n13

Rosenblum, Karen, and Toni-Michelle Travis, 172
Rosenfeld, Michael, 1
Rowe, Amy Carillo, and Adela Licona, 10
Rubin, Lilian, 13, 45, 152, 190n11
Rusbult, C. E., and B. P. Buunk, 138

Same-sex couples, 7, 103–5, 121–24, 154–57
Scott, Joan, 182
Seidman, Steve, 189n5
Seshagiri, Urmila, 170
Sillars, Alan, Linda Roberts, and Tim Dun, 191n2
Skegg, Beverley, 189n3
Smith, Barbara, 82
Smith, Dorothy, 182
Smith, Reger, 6, 166
Smith, Sidonie, and Julia Watson, 182, 185
Snowball sampling, 11–12
Social background, 5
Social difference, 5
Something New, 171
Spickard, Paul, 6, 46, 62, 82
Spillman, Lyn, 49
Staples, Robert, and Boulin Johnson, 7
Stephan, Cookie White, 47, 48
Stewart, Lea, et al., 152
Strong, Bryan, Christine DeVault, and Barbara Sayad, 152
Stryker, Sheldon, 47
Stuart, Irving, and Lawrence Abt, 2
Subjectivity, 8

Tagaki, Dana, 9, 82
Tajfel, Henri, 48
Tannen, Deborah, 152
Tartakov, Carlie, and Gary Tartakov, 11, 63, 64, 70, 100–101, 119–20
Tauber, Mike, Pamela Singh, and Alan Goodman, 172
Taylor, Verta, and Nancy Whittier, 49
Thornton, Michael, 2, 175
Troy, Adam, Jamie Lewis-Smith, and Jean-Philippe Laurenceau, 7

U.S. Census Bureau, 1, 18

Vosburgh, Miriam, and Richard Juliani, 46

Wajcman, Judy, 13
Walter, Roland, 10
Wanzo, Rebecca, 8
Ward, Jane, 9, 82
Waters, Mary, 175, 192n7
Weber, Lynn, 9, 10
West, Candace, and Sarah Fernstermaker, 9
Wilkerson, Isabel, 2
Wood, Julia, 152, 154

Yancey, George, and Richard Lewis, 2, 46
Yuval-Davis, Nira, 4, 50

Zhang, Yuanting, and Jennifer Van Hook, 2, 7, 166
Zinn, Maxine Baca, and D. Stanley Eitzen, 13

About the Author

JILL M. BYSTYDZIENSKI is Professor and Chair of the Department of Women's, Gender and Sexuality Studies at The Ohio State University, author of *Women in Electoral Politics: Lessons from Norway* (1995) and co-editor of *Removing Barriers: Women in Academic Science, Technology, Engineering, and Mathematics* (2006), *Forging Radical Alliances Across Difference: Coalition Politics for the New Millennium* (2001), and *Democratization and Women's Grassroots Movements* (1999).